Mind Management
& Mindfulness

Getting the results that you want in life

a practical guide to
beating anxiety, stress and depression

Anthony Beardsell

Published in 2014 by Excellence Assured Ltd

Copyright © Anthony Beardsell 2014

Anthony Beardsell has asserted his right to be identified as the author of this work in accordance with the Copyright, Designs and Patents Act 1988.

The moral right of the author has been asserted.

All rights reserved

No part of this publication may be reproduced, stored in a retrieval system, or transmitted in any form or by any means, electronic, mechanical, photocopying, recording or otherwise, without the prior permission in writing of the copyright owner.

Excellence Assured Ltd
excellenceassured.com

CONTENTS

Part 1 - Why we think and act as we do

1	Getting your life the way that you want it	2
2	Finding the missing link	7
3	Triune Brain	11
4	Roles and duties of the unconscious mind	14
5	Communicating	42
6	Your power to change	57
7	Our inner saboteur	65
8	Unwanted behaviour. addictions and our saboteur	74
9	Anxiety, stress and depression	86

Part 2 - Beginning to shape your future

10	Values and Beliefs	98
11	Discovering your values	104
12	Identifying the direction of your motivation	115
13	Tuning up your motivation & energising your values	125

Part 3 - Your Mindfulness Programme

14	Mindfulness	134
15	Getting to know your autopilots	161
16	Body and Breath	173
17	Embracing Body and Mind	186
18	The carrot and stick trap	200
19	False beliefs and awareness of your saboteur	215
20	Accepting and befriending your saboteur	234
21	Being compassionate	245
22	Turning towards your future	255
23	Planning your future	259

Part 1 - Why we think and act as we do

INTRODUCTION

Getting your life the way that you want it - Mind Management and Mindfulness

Think about this question: "In what way is my life not yet the way that I want it?"

Reading this book will provide you with the information that you need to understand in simple terms how your mind works, and why your life is not yet the way that you want it. We will go together on a voyage of self-discovery. I will then share with you some practical tools that you can use to make the necessary adjustments in your thinking and behaviours to improve your happiness, success and confidence.

As we work together to improve your awareness of yourself and your mind processes I will be seeking to provide you with some answers to the following questions:

- Why am I so anxious?
- Why does it feel like I am holding myself back?

- Why have I got no energy?
- Why am I not as happy as I would like to be?
- Why do I worry so much?
- How can I be more confident?
- How can I become a better person?
- How can I improve my levels of happiness and success?
- How can I become less stressed?
- How can I improve my relationships?
- How can I develop mind management strategies that improve my levels of happiness, success and health?
- How can I get my life the way that I want it?
- How can I get the results that I want in life?

.....and many more.

Mind Management

The extent of your happiness and current level of success in life largely comes down to your mind management skills.

Having spent many years studying and working with people who are being successful, occasionally having success myself, I have noticed that one of the things that these people consistently do is they manage their mind and unconscious processes really well.

They foster a tremendous relationship between their unconscious processes and their conscious processes and skills. This stands out as being one of the factors that separates them from the rest and this is what I mean by mind management.

There is no doubt that there is a correlation between thinking success and achieving success. Inner success and outer success.

Think about the happiest people that you know, top sports people, top athletes, leading politicians, top people in business, top sales people: there are certain attributes that they all share, certain mindsets that they share and certain habits that they share and that lead them to think slightly differently and create successful results.

Sir Alex Ferguson, ex-Manchester United football manager, says in his autobiography that he was reading the biography of Vince Lombardi, one of the most successful American Football coaches of all time, and as he was reading it he thought "That's me he's writing about, I'm just like Lombardi."

A combination of conscious and unconscious processes

When I talk about unconscious processes, these are the processes that you carry out and that you are not aware of, that are unconscious to you. Anything that you are not immediately aware of is unconscious. Unconscious processes can be behaviours as simple as breathing, lifting your arm, and they can be as complex as driving to work without crashing! Unconscious processes include thought processes, such as recall of memories, knowledge, beliefs and emotions.

Conscious processes are behaviour and thoughts that you are aware of consciously. Such as your interpretation of the words you are reading right now, calculations, planning, deliberate actions.

Think of the mind management skills required to be a great leader, a top tennis player. The elite tennis players are able to control and manage their emotions so that they produce the best tennis when the pressure is at the most intense. They are able, just through watching the toss of the ball on an opponent's serve or the positioning of their body, their backswing, determine where the ball is likely to go and respond in order to produce a return in the blink of an eye. They can't possibly do all of this consciously, can they? Some of it is conscious and most of it is unconscious.

Great leaders know what to do and say under the utmost pressure to produce a successful communication and outcome. They have hundreds of things to consider at any one time but they are able to be calm and decisive. This is not just down to their conscious actions and thoughts, but a combination of conscious and unconscious, almost instinctive responses.

It has been said numerous times that the winner of the 100m olympic gold medal wins the race before they even get on the starting blocks. I think that in a sense this is true and it is a harmonious combination of conscious thoughts and actions with unconscious processes that creates success, happiness and elite performance.

If you are not getting the results that you want in life, if you have behaviours that do not support you, if you are not walking your talk, if you want to be the best in the world in your field, then the answer is the same, improve your mind management skills. Work on your inner world to create your outer successes. Work on the perfect marriage between your unconscious mind and your conscious mind.

By getting to know how you create your thoughts, how you create your actions, how you communicate with yourself and others, by creating in yourself a greater awareness of how you function, you will be able to make better choices, gain better control and thus be able to improve your results. This is where we are going to start our work, in line with our three step success strategy.

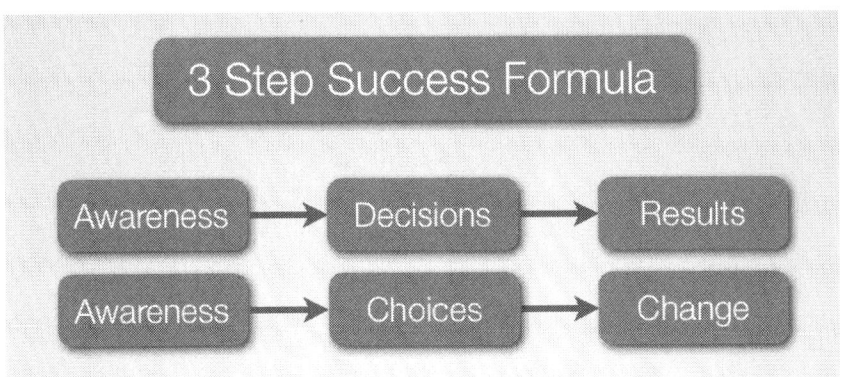

This book contains all the resources that you need to bring about improved self awareness and to help you to start getting the results that you want. There are plenty of practical exercises for you to do in order for you to explore your own thinking and to understand how you are going to improve your life through better mind management and mindfulness.

Additionally, our guided mindfulness exercises are available to you in audio format on our website excellenceassured.com.

CHAPTER 2

Finding the missing link

It was during a four and a half hour drive to work one Monday morning when it clicked for me. I pulled over to the side of the road and looked at the beautiful scenery around me, the sun coming up on the horizon, the mist gently rising from the damp ground. The birds swooping, ducking and diving with abandon in the fields. I slowed down to absorb the scene. The habitual problem-solving thoughts that usually consumed me on Monday morning faded into the background for once as I became starkly aware, for probably the first time, of what was missing in my life.

I'd been playing the game, I'd played it quite well, had a few good victories but they had left me with an empty feeling. I have always been really interested in success and what makes people successful, I have read hundreds and hundreds of books over the years, autobiographies, self help books, business psychology, NLP (Neuro-Linguistic Programming), sales manuals, Seven Habits of Highly Effective People type books. I had learned to apply the techniques in a business and sales environment and discovered that they worked!

I had discovered how to win, twice in successive sales roles I had risen to the top of the salesforce, the second time it took me less than two years to achieve record sales figures. I was quickly promoted to management and then senior management roles, where happily I was able to continue to generate successful results and income for my employers and myself.

Was this the life of The Wolf of Wall Street, Gordon Gekko? Hardly. I was successful in my field, more successful than the people working around me but not exactly an international superstar! I earned good money for the work that I did but nothing particularly obscene. My sphere of influence gradually grew but it never extended further than the company that I was working for.

One thing that has always been important to me is **consideration for others**. I was always ethical at work. always acted with the clients best interest at heart. I was always honest, never sold anything to anyone that they didn't need. I treated people who worked with me and latterly for me with dignity. I never wanted to rule the world, I just wanted to do well and do it in the right way.

I worked hard. This was certainly one of the reasons for my success, no great secret there. Hard work normally brings about success. At times of my greatest success I worked very hard, I skipped holidays, worked weekends and evenings, spent three to four nights per week in hotels, travelled a thousand miles per week on congested British motorways. I developed a singular purpose for my life, to be successful, this was my focus and in the early part of my career I never took my eye off this objective.

Was I enjoying my success? Well, this is the thing, I thought that I was. I enjoyed the thought of being the top sales person, I enjoyed looking at my payslips and my bank statements were showing positive for the first time in my life. I enjoyed reaching my objectives, I savoured my success, for a couple of minutes....then my mind moved on to what came next. New year, new targets, everything starts over again. I have to say that at times I was so wrapped up in my objectives, in the workload that came with achieving my objectives, that I did not look up at all, I had my head down and never looked up.

I lived for at least ten years like this, head down, focussed on my objectives. One of my highest values is **having fun at work**, so I was determined to have fun as well as working hard. As a sales person, I smiled through my days, this brought me energy and won me friends and customers. As a manager I smiled and joked until the company finally wiped the smile off my face. As a senior manager it was made clear to me that smiling and joking at work was not appropriate. Year after year I hit my targets and achieved my objectives, the sacrifices seemed worthwhile, I was seduced by my own dreams and the world around me, society, culture appeared to positively encourage this self deception.

Relaxing was proving tricky, I have to admit. My brain was working overtime, planning future events, working out solutions, running over and re-running over conversations that I had in meetings, phone calls, planning conversations that I expected to have in future meetings to ensure that they went my way. There was not enough time in the day to do all that I had to do, so I worked evenings and weekends to compensate. When I did take physical time away from work my mind was still at it, whirring away, planning, reviewing. I self medicated - a pack of beer seemed to do the trick until the morning when the mind started up again!

I look back now and realise that I had started to feel tired during the day. This had never happened to me before, I was always full of energy. It was no surprise that this was happening, beer in the evening, lack of sleep, overworked brain, and I wasn't living and working to my highest values.

Whenever I took time out for a bit of sport I would go on a guilt trip. I would play a round of golf and feel guilty about all of the work chores that I was neglecting. I played golf and thought of work. Maybe if I spent my round of golf planning my meetings in my head then I wouldn't feel so guilty? Self deception.

Reading for leisure, became problematic, in fact reading at all became problematic. I loved reading but if I was reading, then I wasn't working on my backlog of work related tasks. I would read a page of a book and then have to reread it as I realised that I hadn't actually been concentrating on what I was reading. I would read a paragraph, deliberately concentrating and then my mind would be off again, planning, reviewing. I would give it up as a bad job, watching TV seemed to be more effective in distracting me.

I began to spend meetings distracted in my mind. I would be listening and talking but my mind would be off somewhere else, working on what I was doing next, prioritising my tasks. I loved having the opportunity to train and coach others, this would keep my mind fully occupied, I could have fun and at the same time it was working on one of my highest values, **contributing, adding value**.

During this time I thought that I was happy, I was being successful so I must have been happy, right? I was achieving my objectives, my targets and my goals so of course I assumed that I must be happy. Plenty of people envied me, wanted what I appeared to have. I was doing everything that it said in the books and it was working, this was the way that it was supposed to be, wasn't it? Why was it then that I started spending my work hours wishing that I could be relaxing, and the hours that I had the opportunity to relax, feeling guilty about not working? It was beginning to dawn on me that I was resenting work, seeing it all as a chore. How could this be? What was I missing?

CHAPTER 3

Triune Brain

In order for you to get a good grasp of what we are talking about when we speak of mind management it is worth taking a look at how our brain has developed throughout our evolution.

There are lots of examples of how various species have evolved physically and mentally to suit their environment, to allow them to survive and thrive. Look at how some species of fish are able to change colour in order to blend into the seabed, how creatures have the power of sting to attack and to defend against larger creatures in their environment. How animals have been born with the ability, unique to them, to allow them to carry out complex mental processes in order to find and eat food. Of course if a species does not evolve then it dies.

Let's have a look at a bit of science momentarily. In the 1960s the American physician and neuroscientist Dr Paul MacLean proposed a model of the evolution of the human brain that he called the Triune Brain. This model helps us to understand the basics of how we think and create our world.

The Reptilian Complex

Essentially MacLean identified that the brain has evolved in three stages. The original part of our brain is the Reptilian Complex. This part of the brain is inherited from reptiles, thus the label "Reptilian". When I say inherited, we are talking millions and millions of years ago of course. Think for a moment about the world of the reptile, it was pretty basic: eat or be eaten. We are talking about a brain built for survival. This part of the brain helps us with our basic needs: breathing, maintaining our heart beat and other vital functions.

This reptilian part of our brain is responsible for our fight or flight response. Back in those days the reptiles' brain helped them to survive by weighing up any situation and deciding whether they should stand their ground and fight or save themselves by running off. We know it now as an instinctual response.

Limbic System

Then, over the next couple of hundred millions of years a second part of our brain evolved, this is called the Limbic System. This part of the brain we inherited from mammals and was originally responsible for the motivation and emotion involved in feeding, reproductive behaviour, and parental behaviour. This is now the home of our emotions and value judgements, deeply unconscious within us. You normally don't decide to get fearful, do you? It just happens. You don't sit there and think "I know, I'm going to get angry" you just get angry, don't you?

The Limbic system takes care of more complex processes than the Reptilian Complex as required to survive and thrive as mammals through evolution. Essentially this part of the brain now fits snugly on top of the original reptilian brain.

Neocortex

The third and final addition comes in the shape of our Neocortex, you will be familiar with this part of your brain as this is the part that you use for doing your conscious thinking. We use it for planning, logic, working out solutions to problems and putting things in order and sequence. This part fits on top of the Limbic System rather like a bicycle helmet and is the bit that you generally see when you look at pictures of the brain, with gentle ripples in it.

Simplifying this a bit then, the Reptilian Complex and the Limbic System, the oldest parts of the brain perform our unconscious functions. We are not aware of our breathing most of the time, we do not have to breathe deliberately, our unconscious Reptilian brain does that for us. We do not deliberately heal our wounds consciously, do we? Our body produces the right chemicals and takes care of that for us, that is the Reptilian brain functioning. We are not consciously producing our emotions of anger, fear, sadness, hurt and guilt, they are unconsciously developed in our Limbic system, we become *aware* of them via our conscious thought processes.

The Neocortex is responsible for our conscious thought processes. This is the human part of our brain and where amongst other things we identify a "self" image. When we have a problem to solve we use this conscious part of the brain to run through the options and find the best solution; we are also able to think rationally in order to plan events for our future using this conscious process.

Let's think about it then as a conscious mind and an unconscious mind working together to serve us, to allow us to survive, to grow, to heal, to learn, to change, to protect us, to enable us to achieve our objectives, whatever we decide that they are.

CHAPTER 4

Roles and duties of the unconscious mind

I am sure that you are more familiar with your conscious mind than you are with your unconscious mind. Of course the conscious mind is where awareness lives, so that makes sense. We can however bring what is unconscious into the light of awareness in order to make improvements.

Notice now the feeling of your left foot, what is it doing? Is it resting on the floor, sofa or relaxing gently in the air? You were not aware of your left foot before I mentioned it, were you? Not consciously anyway. By bringing your attention to it you were able to bring it into your awareness and notice how it feels. You are then able to change the position of the foot, the weight that you are placing on it in order to make it feel more comfortable. This is the approach that we will assist you in taking so that you are able to make positive changes throughout your life. Sounds simple, doesn't it? Well, that is because it is!

Your unconscious mind works with patterns and symbols

The unconscious mind keeps things as simple as possible, remember, flight or fight, breathing, healing, survival. It recognises patterns and symbols from the information and data that it receives via our senses. So, you smell something, smell the air around you now, what do you smell? What does that smell remind you of? Chance are that you are in a familiar environment, so you may have to pay careful attention to the smells around you at the moment. Can you smell your clothing? Any food smells? Can you smell any plants around you? Anything else? If you can smell your clothing, does it smell of washing powder, or can you smell the fabric?

How do you know specifically that it is that particular thing that you can smell? You know the smell of wool, don't you? If you smell wool then how do you know that it is wool? You must know that it is wool because you have smelled it before and learned to label that smell as wool. In fact you have probably had quite a few instances when you have smelled wool, so you have involuntarily programmed your unconscious mind to recognise that smell and to associate it with wool. Your unconscious mind processes various smells at any one time and when it notices the patterns in the smells as the same as those that you previously labelled wool, it notifies the conscious mind that the smell is "wool". This is a really useful asset since it obviously saves you the time of finding a new label for everything all the time!

Thinking on a different level. The grand masters of chess are able to use this same process to their advantage in games of chess. They recognise patterns in the order and sequence of chess pieces on the chess board to enable them to predict what they need to do to give them a successful outcome in that game, what moves to make and in which order to bring about a win. They do not need consciously to think through every combination of possible moves, they just use their knowledge stored unconsciously to predict intuitively what they need to do. Based on past games of chess that they have experienced they have built up a huge volume of patterns and sequences at the unconscious level associated with chess moves, and so their unconscious mind relates the current game patterns to similar patterns from the past to let them "instinctively" and intuitively know the right move to make.

In the same way elite tennis players are able to predict where a ball is going to go based on the patterns that their unconscious mind picks up from seeing the movements of the other player and how they toss the ball on their serve.

Our dreams are unconscious too. We don't consciously construct our dreams but often when we dream we dream sequences of thoughts, pictures, sounds and feelings that reflect certain things that may be going on in our lives. This is our unconscious mind at work. Many years after I left my last place of employment, having not thought about that environment for some time I met an ex-colleague for a chat. We didn't talk about the past, we were chatting about our present lives and work and about what we were planning for the future, however that night I dreamed about going back to work for that old employer and woke up in a cold sweat! That was my unconscious mind at work, recognising patterns and symbols from the present, relating them to the past and representing them to me in the form of my dreams.

Most of our learning is unconscious. We take in information consciously, through our senses: we read, we watch videos, we listen to audios. We process the information using our unconscious mind. When we read something new our unconscious mind tries to enable us to make sense of it by relating it to something that we are familiar with. It tries to spot patterns in the information that it recognises and when it sees one, it says to itself, "ah, I see, this is similar to ....." and it communicates this to our conscious mind to seek approval and confirmation. This is why it is easier to retain information on a subject where you have some previous knowledge of that subject or a similar one. The unconscious mind is easily able to recognise the patterns and store them alongside the other similar things. When you read or learn something that is completely new to you then it may take several reviews before you are able to recall that information and relate it to other pieces of knowledge as the unconscious mind struggles to find comparable patterns and symbols.

Think of children's toys where you match shapes to holes and put the shape through the related hole. This is programming our unconscious mind to recognise the shapes. After doing this for a while as a child we become able to do it without thinking until we come across a shape or hole that we do not recognise. Then we will have to sit and think about it for a bit and maybe experiment placing the shape near various holes until we find the matching hole.

The unconscious mind stores memories

You know when you are trying to remember a name, and it is on the tip of your tongue? You know that you know it but you can't quite remember it, it's really frustrating, isn't it? The more that you try to remember it the more frustrating it gets. Then some time later you think about the same thing and the name is just there, simple and easy as that. What is going on there? Names are stored in our unconscious mind, memories are stored in our unconscious mind. They must be, mustn't they? Otherwise we would be able to remember them straight away. In fact if memories were stored in our conscious mind, then we would be constantly thinking about all of our events in the past, all of them, constantly. Thinking about that is enough to make your mind go pop!

We hear a name, we maybe see the name written down and because it is important to us, or because we hear and see the name several times we send a message to the unconscious mind that "I want to remember this." When we use a name again and again it is easy to remember and it takes no effort to recall it but if we don't use it for a while, then it gets more and more tricky to retrieve it and we actually have to go consciously in search of it in our memory bank (our unconscious mind).

Whilst we are talking about a name specifically, the name is a memory. It may just be words *or* it may have a picture associated with it if you have seen that person and put a face to the name. In fact, the more information that you have associated with the name the easier it is for you to recall the memory from your unconscious mind.

If you have a smell associated with a memory, a label, a picture, a sound and a feeling, then you will be able to use one part of the memory to pull back the rest of it into your conscious thought.

Think about your last holiday now. Please indulge me for a moment. Think about your last holiday. What came first, a picture, a sound, a smell, a feeling? For me it is normally a picture and I can use the picture to pull back memory fragments that include feelings, sounds, smells and tastes. I went to Tenerife and when I see the word Tenerife, it brings back a series of pictures, sounds, feelings, smells and tastes, my memories.

This reminds us that our unconscious mind uses symbols and patterns. By recalling one part of a memory my unconscious mind recognises it and delivers to my conscious mind a whole raft of associated information, thus the pictures, sounds, feelings etc.

One way of **improving your memory** therefore is to associate pictures, sounds and feelings to words. For example, if you think of the word "rabbit", the word itself is not easily recallable if it is mixed in with thirty other words that you may try to memorise, however if you visualise a rabbit, and see it hopping around, imagine the feel of its fur, then you will easily be able to remember the word.

Now, here's an important point. You want to **make a positive impact when you meet people**, right? There is much more chance of this happening if you make someone *feel* good about themselves. As Maya Angelou said "People may forget what you say, people may forget what you do but nobody will ever forget how you make them feel." What is more, all sales people amongst you, it will make you more memorable to them.

Memories are stored according to time

The unconscious mind stores some memories in a general piggy-bank of memories and it stores other memories according to time. Memories such as words are stored with no reference to time. I'm sure that you can't remember the time when you learned the meaning of the word "rabbit"! However memories of things like events are stored in your own personal timeline in your unconscious mind.

Think of something that happened last week, an event. Now think of something that happened six months ago. Now think of something that happened five years ago. You will notice differences between the memories and you may notice that they are stored in order, in a line. Of course, the event that happened five years ago may be less easy to recall vividly than the one that happened last week, however that is not always the case, is it? There are certain memories of events that happened many years ago that may still be absolutely real in your memory and you can recall them as if they happened yesterday.

One of the things that helps with recall is the number of times that a memory is recalled, the other is the amount of sensory information that you associated with the memory at the time. Sensory information is information that we take in through our senses, visual, auditory, kinaesthetic (feeling), olfactory (smell), gustatory (taste). Another thing that helps with recall is the way that the memory made you feel at the time, which you may have been aware of consciously. Additionally having emotions associated with a memory will make the memory more powerful.

The ease of recall of a memory does not alter the place of the memory in your timeline though, does it? The thing that you thought of that happened five years ago may have been much more significant in your life than the thing that you remembered six months ago, however you can still tell that it happened further in your past. Why is that? It is because your unconscious mind stores memories according to time. You may well experience events further in the past as coming to you from further away from you as you think about them. In fact if you really think about it, you can go back through your life's events in your head like watching a DVD on rapid rewind.

Interestingly, your personal timeline does not only go back into your past; it stretches away into your future as well. You can think of things that you expect or want to happen next week, in six months time, in five years time. These may also be stored as "memories" in your unconscious mind. Think about something now that you expect to happen in your life next week. You can associate imaginary pictures with this event, you can imagine yourself in the picture or looking at the picture through your own eyes, you can hear sounds around you in the event, you can hear yourself talking, you can imagine yourself touching things and feelings that you may have in the event. Again, the more sensory information that you include in the memory, the more real it becomes for you.

As you do this process, your unconscious mind is listening to your conscious instruction to create the memory and it is picking up symbols and patterns from past events that it can associate with what you might expect to see, hear, feel in the future event. This results in the rather lifelike future memory that you can experience when you think about it (now). This is your conscious mind and your unconscious mind working in harmony.

The domain of your emotions

How are you feeling right now? You may have had the thought of, "I'm feeling OK" or "I'm feeling good" or "I'm feeling relaxed". What constitutes feeling "OK" for you? What has to be happening in order for you to feel "OK"? In fact does anything have to be happening for you to feel "OK"? Maybe "OK" is just what you feel when there is nothing bad happening? Did you notice how you were feeling before I asked the question? You may have had a sense of how you were feeling, if you have been feeling particularly bad today, then you may have had more than just a sense of it, it may be constantly playing on your mind, in your conscious thoughts.

Now go deeper into this feeling. What emotions are there? Do you feel any joy, any enthusiasm, any fear, any anger? Maybe there are little bits of emotions there lingering on from events that have occurred earlier today or further in your past? Notice that you have to really think about this in order to get the answers to my questions. You have to search deep into your unconscious in order to discover what is there.

Emotions are stimulated by events that take place and how you respond to the events. Emotions are stirred up in the unconscious mind, they are a response by your unconscious mind to events. Your unconscious mind provides an automatic reaction to events based on how it interprets the events and in the way that it calculates will best support you, this is the intention but it does not always work that way.

Remember again that the unconscious mind reacts with a flight or fight response to events and it learns through patterns and symbols. When you are a child people will tell you things like, "do not put your hand over the top of the flame on a lighted candle." It makes sense now but to the ears and eyes of a child things are not quite so clear cut. Life is an adventure to a child, children are curious, really curious, flames are interesting, spectacular, enticing, alluring. As a child, you are tempted by the suggestion. You put your hand over the flame....and you quickly realise that people were right!

You feel pain, you are conditioned to understand that pain is bad, your conscious mind sends messages to your unconscious mind that this is a lesson that needs to be heeded for the future, flames cause pain. The response that we want is flight not fight in this sort of circumstance. The unconscious mind logs the event with all the data for future reference.

Next time you see a lighted candle you know automatically not to go too near it. You can feel the fear, the pain even by just thinking about touching the space just above the flame. Your unconscious mind is serving you with the emotion of fear based upon past experience and instruction that you have given it. Pain is bad, flames are dangerous and painful.

It depends on the impact of your experience as to how deeply you may have been affected by the pain. If you suffer severe burns, then the messages that are received by your unconscious mind are hugely significant. Your unconscious mind is going to make absolutely sure that if you are ever presented with the same situation in the future you avoid it at all costs. In fact your unconscious mind is going to be constantly looking out for patterns and symbols in your thoughts and in your experiences that may possibly result in the same painful outcome. This is where **phobias and nightmares** result. The problem is that the unconscious mind is not able to distinguish between specific sensory data. It sees signs for potential pain and it screams out to you, "back off!!" You experience the feelings of fear.

Any sign of a naked flame may be enough to bring about a crippling fear response, even if you are nowhere near it. You may even suffer nightmares or flashbacks as your mind relives the event. Fear will come with them.

Think about the fear of spiders. So many people are afraid of spiders, hardly anyone has been bitten by a spider, but the communal message is "spiders bite, they are horrible crawly little things." The unconscious mind listens to these messages over and over again and it is conditioned to present people with a fear response to spiders. The mere sight of a live spider is enough to send people into frenzied panic. Completely irrational fear but very real to anyone with a phobia for spiders.

Notice that these fears, these emotions are automatic, there is no logic or thinking involved at this stage in producing the emotion. It is only when we have had time to think and weigh up the situation normally that we consider the real danger, using our conscious, rational resources and the fear dissipates.

It works the same way for anger. When the "red mist" descends, it seems to come from nowhere, it seems uncontrollable, it takes over the entire system and it can be sparked by the smallest of things. This is the fight response, delivered by the unconscious mind, a direct response, a response to allow survival in a world where only the strongest survive. The thing is that the world is not like that most of the time anymore, thankfully.

Talking science again, this response comes from the Amygdala, part of the Limbic System, part of our unconscious mind. Sensory information bypasses our Neocortex, there is no logical response involved, it goes straight to the Amygdala and the response is anger.

Maintains and generates habits

Bring to mind something in your life that you are good at, a skill that you have acquired. It may involve working with other people in some way, it may be something to do with your work, it could be a sport, anything. Have you always been good at it? I mean *always*? The chances are that you have had to work at it, build your skill and you will have gone through several stages of development to get to where you are now.

How many of the actions or thoughts involved with the skill do you actually have to think about in order to carry them out? How many of the actions involved have become "natural" to you? Much of our behaviour comes naturally to us over time, we carry out the behaviour unconsciously. We generate habits that allow us to complete the behaviour, and thought processes, without having to actually think about it and plan our outcomes consciously. It is a good job that it works this way if you think about it otherwise we would inundated by thoughts and continuously in a state of overwhelm!

Think about the skills involved in standing up and walking, I imagine that you have become pretty good at that over time, and it hasn't always been that way. You probably do not have to think consciously anymore about putting your hands in a certain place in order to push yourself out of your chair. You do not have to think about how far apart to place your feet, where to put your weight in order to make sure that you do not fall over, which foot to place in front of the other in order to move forward, which muscles to move, how you move your hands and arms to gain momentum and maintain balance. All of this is completed unconsciously, all of this has become simple habitual behaviour.

We were all born with the ability to learn how to walk, we were not born with the skills needed to do it, we had to go through a painful learning process in order to gain the skills and we can now do it without thinking about it. With any skill that you possess the process will have been similar.

Obviously lying in a cot has its limitations, and so we develop a desire and a need to get up and move around. We see people around us walking about and because this is a skill that we desire we copy their specific movements and behaviour, these are our role models. We try on the behaviour and go through a trial and error process of first of all pushing ourselves into an upright position so that we get a better view. We learn to crawl, we learn to fall over, we learn to stumble and we learn to walk. We are driven through the fear process by our need and desire. At first it takes all of our concentration and we still can not do it, but we build the skill, complex movement by complex movement. Sitting up becomes second nature, we are ready to move on to the next level, adding more unconscious movements bit by bit until we accomplish our goal. You can now walk, hold a conversation, play on your phone and avoid bumping into lamp posts, all without thinking about it!

Your unconscious mind cannot distinguish between good behaviours and bad behaviours. It relies on your conscious decision making and serves you according to your conscious instruction.

If you carry out any behaviour a sufficient number of times then it will become an unconscious habit for you. The more frequently that you perform the behaviour the quicker the habit becomes unconscious for you and the easier it is to replicate. Habits can appear hard to break because the behaviour has become so unconscious that it almost seems to become part of who you are. Your beliefs about yourself and your values become associated with this behaviour.

Problematic behaviour and thinking occurs due to this process of habit making. I discussed with you that I had become consumed with problem-solving thoughts. Every minute of the day I was planning forward, reviewing past events, decisions and conversations. This started off as a very useful tool for me, it allowed me to think that I was always one step ahead, I never missed an opportunity, I could handle more work than anyone else around me, I was always "on my game". I practised it continuously so I became very good at it and I could do it without deliberately setting aside an intention to do it. Then it became habitual, I could not stop doing it. My mind just would not switch off, I was doing it when I was trying to go to sleep, I was doing it when I should have been listening to other people and I was doing it in my leisure time, it was interrupting me when I was reading. I was not doing it deliberately, and I found it tricky at the time to deliberately stop doing it. I had created a need and desire to learn this method of thinking, I learned how to do it, I could do it easily, I began doing it automatically, it became a habit that I could not switch off and it started to cause me problems.

Learning and repetition

The process of learning is habit creation. There may be things that you are reading here that you can identify with, things that you were not aware of before, but you can identify with them now that they have been brought to your attention. This is the first step in learning, it starts with awareness. Sometimes you do not know what you do not know until you are made aware of it. You remain as they say unconsciously incompetent. Awareness highlights to you all of the things that you were unaware of and it highlights to you that you are not very good at it, or things are not the way that you want them, you become consciously incompetent.

You then enter the second stage of learning which is to practice what you want, not what you do not want, you follow instruction, you learn from role models, mentors, you enter the stage of trial and error. Gradually you build your skills, you begin to realise what works and what does not work, you build a set of values and beliefs around these skills, you really need to concentrate to do it and when you concentrate you are able to create successful results. This is the stage of being consciously competent. We are going to provide you with the tools that you need to complete this stage in your mind management.

The third stage of learning is moving to unconscious competence. You practise and practise your skills, you begin to automate the process. Gradually, bit by bit you create a series of habits in thinking and behaviour that allow you to carry out the skills unconsciously, automatically. As you develop and practise your mind management skills you will develop new behaviours, you will design your habits and change your habits to suit the way that you wish to live your life. Your new behaviours will become automatic for you over time, you will develop new strategies, beliefs and values around how you want your life and that will support you going forward. **This is how you will change and how you will get your life the way that you want it.**

Repetition is the mother of learning, repetition is your instruction to your unconscious mind that "This is important, please remember this." You reinforce your learning and strengthen your habits through repetition. If you lay your tools down and let your skills become idle then your unconscious mind sees this as an instruction to concentrate on something else. The patterns and symbols that it uses to produce unconscious success will fade and become mixed with other symbols and patterns, you will move back in your learning cycle to conscious incompetence, you try to use your skills and you realise that you can not do it as well as you used to. You will then need to reapply conscious thinking to regenerate the old behaviour as you used to have it, only this time it may be different.

Path of least resistance

Human beings are built to grow and develop. Your unconscious mind is there to serve you in this purpose. Bearing this in mind the unconscious mind is all about efficiency, it assists you in freeing up space in your conscious thinking for making important decisions, taking in information, digesting it, weighing up options, planning a better life, working out ways of better serving other people. It takes over routine thinking and behaviour and it allows you to develop more complex ways of thinking and behaving. This facilitates your growth and development.

Forever in search of a quicker and better route to giving you what you want, your unconscious mind will seize on any opportunity to take a short cut. It works on the principle of least effort. This can be a good thing and it can also be a bad thing of course.

One of the tactics that the unconscious mind uses is a process of grouping information, otherwise known as chunking. We are able to put data and information together in strings, groups or chunks in order for us to process and remember it better. Think of how you memorise numbers, say your phone number to yourself. The chances are that you have memorised the number in chunks of two, three or four numbers. For example, 0121 358 9971. Remembering 11 different numbers in a sequence is tricky, grouping the numbers into chunks of three or four all of a sudden makes remembering them a lot easier.

Going back to remembering our word "rabbit". Let's say that we want to remember the words rabbit, frog and seagull. We could use the tactic as before of picturing the individual animals, one by one, or better we could imagine all three sitting together on our sofa in front of the fire. By grouping the animals together in our imagination we only need to remember one scene rather than three.

This chunking of memories occurs constantly in order to make recall easier for us. We can pick up the thread of a memory by consciously searching for it. Think about what happened in your life last Tuesday. What did you do? You may need to cycle back through the days to get there. As you remember this you can now start to remember other things that happened that day. You may remember who you spoke with, what you spoke about, how the conversation made you feel, even your emotions. Our unconscious mind recognises the request for information, it picks up the thread of the memory through recognising the pattern in the request and it reveals more and more content as we continue to concentrate on the memory. It had chunked the memories together and stored them as a group, the more threads of thought that you produce in association with the memory the more information will be revealed. This is how people are able to remember very detailed information associated with events in the past using hypnosis, and other memory regression techniques, the police have used this in the past to generate photo-fit pictures of criminals from the memories of victims and passers-by.

You learn a new skill. You learn it deliberately, a process the end result of which gives you what you want. You then sit down to assess the process to see if you can do it more quickly, more efficiently, with fewer moving parts, with less energy, for less cost. You cut out the middle men, you buy new machinery, new tools, you find ways to create the same or better results with fewer people involved. This is progress, this brings about growth. Sometimes we get carried away with this type of efficiency saving and we take it too far. We start emailing customers rather than picking up the phone or popping round for a cup of tea, we shed expertise in our companies because we are cutting staff costs, we stop listening to people's needs and beliefs because it is easier to just tell them what we want.

The intention may be right for us but sometimes we develop shortcuts which harm us.

We do the same thing with our habits. We find a way of loving someone so that it makes them feel special, we pay them attention, we listen, we touch them in the right way, we say the right things...and then it all seems like too much effort, we stop paying the right level of attention, we don't listen because we think that we have heard it all before, we think that they know how we feel about them so we stop telling them that we love them. Shortcuts to poorer relationships.

We call it taking things for granted. Essentially it is relying on our unconscious automatic processes to deliver our results without applying our conscious logical thinking. It is laziness and our unconscious mind cuts corners where it can because it is looking for the path of least resistance. This could in some ways explain the lottery mentality that is pervading society. People want something for nothing.

Represses memories and negative emotions

The highest intention and purpose of your unconscious mind is to serve you by protecting you, ensure survival. Life is full of seasons, good and bad. Things may occur in your life that give a shock to your system; you may experience trauma, significant events that represent to you a real threat to your survival. Often these events bring about a high level of negative emotion, your unconscious mind recognises the event as a threat and it triggers the fight or flight response. It wants you to know in no uncertain terms that you are under threat. We experience great anger (fury), fear (terror), sadness, hurt, guilt, a combination or all of these emotions.

In circumstances like this, these negative emotions are necessary, they may very well provoke a reaction that ensures your survival and they also form part of the healing process, another function of the unconscious mind. It is quite natural on the death of a loved one to feel great sadness, anger and guilt for a while.

Over time our our emotions usually subside, one of the reasons for this is that the memory becomes more distant, other things, bits of information and data take over our attention and dilute our thoughts. Another reason is that hopefully we work through the emotion in our conscious thoughts, we process our thoughts, use logic, recognise the negative emotions, value their purpose for us and move on. For some people this process involves coaching, counselling or therapy. It is sometimes easier to process your thoughts by speaking to someone about them.

Problems can occur when we do not properly work through and process negative emotions. If an event remains unprocessed and we simply decide to ignore our emotions, then they may fade away, but the chances are that they will be back! The emotion is unresolved at the unconscious level, the unconscious mind re-presses the emotion to allow us to function and it waits for a suitable time to represent the emotion to us so that we can resolve it.

Take someone who has suffered physical abuse. This will probably lead to a huge build up of anger, fear and maybe guilt. When the abuse stops the emotions may gradually fade into the background but without therapy or adequate internal processing they will remain unresolved. As this person goes through life they may well experience regular unwarranted levels of negative emotion as a reaction to small, almost insignificant events. This happens as a result of the old repressed emotions from past events rising to the surface. It can lead to that person committing crime, self harming, and illnesses like depression.

The unconscious mind will recognise that the emotions remain unresolved and it will wait for what it judges to be an appropriate moment, when it will represent them to the person in order for them to be resolved. What we think logically might be an appropriate moment is not necessarily how the unconscious mind sees it. The unconscious mind is constantly paying attention to the threads of thought, the information that is received through the senses, to identify moments to get the emotions resolved. This is one reason why you can be minding your own business, even relaxing when all of a sudden you get flashbacks of past events and begin to get emotional.

Feeling emotions is a natural response to events and is beneficial as long as the emotion is in proportion to the event. If we ignore our emotions then they can build up and up. In this case we are in effect carrying the emotions around with us in a backpack, projecting them onto other people, we become a live volcano of emotion waiting to erupt.

Your unconscious mind runs and preserves the body

In line with its highest intention of survival the unconscious mind is in charge of looking after the physical integrity of our body. It is in charge of the production and distribution of chemicals in our system that heal us when we are poorly, that contribute to the feelings of happiness and fear and that provide us with our energy. Our unconscious mind takes benefit from exercise, the input of oxygen, food and liquid in order to produce the right chemicals and distribute them to all areas of our body. Our unconscious mind is like the middleman between our conscious mind and our body, it translates thoughts via chemicals into results in our body.

What is it that ensures that you continue to breathe when you are asleep? When you fell over as a child and cut your knee or your arm, what was it that produced the right chemicals to create the scab as protection for the open wound? How did your body know to do that? How did it notice where exactly the wound was? How did your body know exactly how that piece of skin was before you fell over, such that the wound is now invisible?

One of my clients recently told me about her brother who became ill and had catastrophic organ failure. His liver was destroyed and she was told that he had a less than two percent chance of surviving. He survived and his body started repairing itself. According to his doctors his liver has started to repair itself back to full health. Surely this is magic? How on earth can that happen? We are only now beginning to really understand the chemical processes involved in maintaining the body and the connection between the body and the mind. One thing is sure though, there are billions and billions of neurological connections in our body and our unconscious mind is at the heart of its communication. It must be because we don't do it consciously, do we?

Illnesses generally occur when we are run down. Have you ever developed a cold when you have been through a time of particularly intensive activity, when you have been feeling tired? Illnesses are a sign that our body is feeling uncomfortable, they are a sign from our body that we need to look after ourselves, slow down a bit, have a rest. If we do not heed this message, then our body may well enforce rest upon us by the illness getting worse.

Joe Simpson was descending the remote 6,344 metre (20,813 foot) Siula Grande mountain in Peru when he slipped and broke his leg. In the dark and using 150-foot lengths of ropes, his climbing partner proceeded to lower him down the face of the mountain towards the glacier below. Unwittingly, Simpson was lowered over the edge of a cliff. Unable to haul Simpson's dead weight back up again, and concerned that he too was sliding off the cliff, his climbing partner cut the rope.

Simpson plummeted down the mountain and straight into a crevasse, landing on a shelf deep in the crevasse. He was still alive but completely unable to climb out of the crevasse due to his broken leg and the overhanging walls above him, so he decided that he had no option but to descend further into the crevasse.

At day break his climbing partner descended the mountain and went in search of Simpson, however seeing no sign of him and realising that he must have fallen into the crevasse, he assumed that he was dead and decided to return to their camp.

Simpson eventually spotted an opening in the crevasse that he could get to via a steep snow slope and he proceeded to climb out. At this stage he was five miles from camp and separated from it by a maze of further crevasses. He was unable to walk due to his broken leg, and he had no food and no water.

In his book, *Touching the Void*, Simpson recounts in vivid detail how he shuffled and crawled the five miles back to camp. It took him three days. Something deep inside of him kept motivating him through the pain in his leg to move forward. Somehow he survived three nights and three days of intense cold and summoned sufficient energy to continue on his journey back to camp. He should have died. He remembers hearing an inner voice guiding him and encouraging him. He dare not sleep in the open for fear of freezing to death.

"...don't sleep, don't sleep, not here. Keep going. Find a slope and dig a snow hole...don't sleep." The voice said.

"Get moving....don't lie there....stop dozing....move!" The voice knew that if he rested he may never get going again.

In agony, he crawled his way over a crevasse riddled glacier, eating snow, melting it with his breath.

He finally arrived back to camp, just as his climbing partner was about to leave to head back to civilization. He was so convinced that Joe was dead that he had burned Joe's clothes. It is an amazing story, a feat of perseverance, survival and determination. What was that voice? What was the thing that kept him alive? What kept him awake and motivated? The unconscious mind is a powerful friend indeed.

In charge of perceptions

It was 1986 and I was spending a week living with a Spanish family in Barcelona, part of a reciprocal agreement where we would host the Spanish boy later in the year. The family were very generous and hospitable to me and they laid on various trips and excursions during this week to keep me entertained. 1986 was the last time that Halley's Comet passed by earth, a very rare occasion indeed and one that is only repeated every 75-76 years. The Spanish boy was really interested in astronomy, he had pictures of planets and space rockets on the walls of his bedroom. One of the main events of the week was to get up in the middle of the night to view Halley's Comet as it made its closest overhead pass. This event was greatly anticipated by my friend and his family.

We set off in the car in the dead of night to the hilltop where the homage to Halley's Comet was taking place. As there were hundreds of cars parked by the side of the road, we parked near the bottom of the hill and joined the hoards trudging up the dusty path to the improvised viewing point at the top of the hill. I was curious rather than excited. It was the first that I had heard of this comet and I had never seen a comet before, so I was looking forward to seeing the show. Apparently it was going to be spectacular.

There was quite a crowd at the viewing point, people were talking animatedly, staring into space even though the comet was not expected for an hour or so yet. It was a calm, warm night with a smattering of clouds, not sufficient to completely obscure the view I was told. Some people had binoculars, a few had big, long telescopes and cameras with telescopic lenses but we would be able to see it with the naked eye, which made it unique amongst comets. I was yawning away and wondering why we had got there so early when we could have been sleeping.

The crowd grew, as did the noise level in the crowd as the time approached for the arrival of the comet. There were loud shouts from some people around us with the big machinery. It was on its way.

I think that I saw it. I think that I caught a glimpse. The cloud had thickened and it was not easy to be actually sure. I prepared myself for a better view as it got closer, *there must be more?*

People turned their heads away from the sky and started addressing each other, some hugged.

"Did you see it?" It was my Spanish friend.

"Did you see it?" He repeated, louder this time.

I turned towards him, he was wide eyed.

"I think so." I said. "Is that it? Is it gone now?"

"Yes. Wasn't it amazing?" He said.

I stayed silent. *Not really.* I thought.

An hour or so later we made our way back down the hill, to the car and back to bed. Maybe I'll see more next time, in 2061!

Now let's look at this through the eyes of my Spanish friend.

"I can't wait to see Halley's comet. I've been waiting for this evening for so long. It's a once in a lifetime experience, I'm sooo excited. I have been lying awake, looking at the drawings from the last time it visited in 1910, it looks amazing!

It's a shame that we haven't been able to bring the binoculars but Dad was right that it wouldn't be fair for one of us to have the binoculars when we only have one pair. Anyway, it is great to be able to share this with Anthony, I know that he doesn't share my interest in astronomy but I'm sure that he'll be converted once he has seen it.

Fantastic, there are not as many cars here as I thought that there would be, we can quickly park up and get up there early to get a good spot. I'm not missing out on this one. Let's GO!

Great, this is a perfect night for it, there are hardly any clouds and we are going to get a good view. I wish that I was able to borrow one of those big telescopes to see it approaching, still, it doesn't matter.

It must be due any time now. "There! There!" *Someone shouts from the other side of the hill. Oh, yes. I can definitely see something. Yes, there it is, I can make out the tail. There it is! Just like in the drawings. Amazing, it is beautiful. What an experience. Did Anthony see it?*

"Did you see it?" *He turns to me, a puzzled look on his face, yawning. Yawning?!*

Great, he saw it too. Let's talk about what we saw. What? We are going back already? I'm not ready to go back, I just want five more minutes up here, there is so much to discuss."

How is it that two people can experience the same event and come away with different perceptions of that event? Our perceptions allow us to represent and understand our environment, they come from the organisation and interpretation of sensory information. Our perceptions are controlled and maintained by our unconscious mind which performs for us the task of interpreting the sensory information that we take in.

Light strikes the retinas in our eyes and enables vision, hearing involves pressure waves taken in through our ears, odour molecules give us smells. It is not just the receipt of these signals that give us our perception but how we shape them by applying our memories, learning, attention and expectation. This is the duty performed by our unconscious mind.

In the above example I had a very different experience that evening to that of my friend. My memories now of the event will be markedly different to his and these are shaped by the perceptions at the time.

I had no particular interest in astronomy or knowledge in that area, whereas my friend did. He knew what to look for, he was significantly more excited and was paying a great deal more attention than me. We were looking at the same thing and he saw it clearly. I think that I may have seen it. His eyesight was no better than mine, but his knowledge and enthusiasm shaped his experience. For me it was a nice outing, a unique experience and it turned out to be a bit of a damp squib. For him it was a momentous occasion, he enjoyed it from start to finish, every second of it, he was talking about it for the rest of the week.

I had expected to see the comet in crystal clear detail, he knew that it would only be a distant, fleeting sight. Our memories, learning, attention and expectation shaped our experience. Memories, learning, values, beliefs are all stored in and managed by the unconscious mind. Our unconscious minds processed the same sensory information and transmitted perceptions to our conscious minds, different perceptions of the same information.

Take a look at the picture below:

What do you see? Do you see a vase? What else do you see? Anything? When I first looked at the picture I saw the vase, only the vase. I then read that it was also possible to see two heads, side on. I was then able to make out the two heads. The knowledge that I gained gave me a different perception and this perception became conscious to me, I became aware of it.

Enjoys serving and needs clear instructions

In the vase example above, my conscious mind read that there was a picture and that if I looked at it a certain way I could see two heads. My conscious mind gave a clear instruction to my unconscious mind to "Go find the heads." As my unconscious mind knows what a head looks like, it picked up the symbols and patterns in the picture that resembled the heads and it fed the perception to my conscious mind. You may have experienced something similar. Or maybe not!

The instructions that we give to our unconscious mind are all important. We need to be really clear and specific with what we want. Remember that the unconscious mind is prone to taking shortcuts and will seek the simplest solution to give you the outcome that you have requested, it will take the path of least resistance.

Think about the way that you may give instruction to a child. If you say to a child "Be good for me." What does that actually mean? It could means lots of things, couldn't it? It could imply "How's about giving me a nice back massage?" Or "Don't stick your tongue out at people but you can carry on wiping that chocolate on your nice clean sweater!" It is a vague instruction and it may bring about a variety of outcomes.

If you were to say, "sit here quietly and wait for a minute please." This is much more specific, it is absolutely clear what the instruction is and it would be difficult to misunderstand. You are much more likely to get your desired outcome.

If you are learning a really tricky skill, and you practice and practice and practice, you focus entirely on this skill and nothing else, then you are much more likely to develop this skill than if you attempt to learn several similar skills at the same time. Your attention towards developing the skill is clear and obvious, a clear and obvious instruction to the unconscious mind.

If you wish to remember something, then writing that thing down is a clear instruction to the unconscious mind that "This thing is important. I want to remember it." Repetition is really vital to learning for the same reason and as we have discussed, this is how habits form. Some people use mantras to get them in the right frame of mind, saying the same words over and over again until they believe that the words have sunk in at the unconscious level and they become the words.

Your unconscious mind is your friend and your servant. If you give it clear instructions, then it will attempt to deliver the results that you are looking for. Bear in mind that the unconscious mind is in charge of maintaining and preserving the body, so when people look in the mirror and say, "I'm looking tired and old today" how do you think that their unconscious mind will respond? It is unlikely to send the right chemicals out into the system to make us look and feel any better!

Does not process negatives

I was walking through a subway under the river which flows through the center of Melbourne and on the wall of the subway I saw a sign that said "Do not spit". Unfortunately people did not seem to have heeded the instruction as the sign was coated in a thick layer of what appeared to be phlegm! No phlegm on the floor, just on and around the sign on the wall. You can google it and see for yourself if you really want to.

Now, don't think of a blue tree. As you read this, follow my instruction carefully, don't think of a blue tree. Please do what I say. Hopefully you didn't think of a blue tree, did you?

The unconscious mind does not process negatives, your unconscious mind picks up the thread of my request, and it reads blue tree. It works with symbols, and it stores memories and so it provides you with the data that it associates with the words "blue" and "tree" combined. Your conscious mind receives the interpretation of the words in a format that we can understand, a picture.

Before I mentioned not thinking of a blue tree you probably hadn't ever contemplated a blue tree but my words provoked the thought in you and your mind created the possibility. This illustrates the power of influence that we have with our words. Back in the subway in Melbourne I am pretty sure that people had not contemplated spitting at the wall before they read it, the words that they read stimulated the possibility in the minds of the pedestrians, inevitably some reacted. Once the words have been acknowledged we cannot help but to process them and the unconscious mind ignores the negative and provides us with an internal representation of the words.

Think about the warning "It is really icy outside, don't fall." What internal representations does this bring about? It is icy and falling over. When we step outside, what are we going to be focussing on? The possibility of falling over, which makes it much more likely. If you think about not falling over, then you can't help but imagine actually falling over. If you are consciously thinking about falling over, then the unconscious mind can see this is an instruction. In this situation, if we said, "It is icy outside, watch your footing," then that is going to get a much better response because we are going to be thinking about keeping our footing.

People say to children "Don't bite your nails." What response does this provoke in them? Take someone who is trying to quit smoking and they keep saying to themselves, don't think about smoking. Every time they remind themselves not to think about smoking they must consider actually smoking. The unconscious mind needs clear and positive instructions to follow.

Key Points

Most people are aware of the involvement of conscious thinking in their lives and not so aware of their unconscious thinking and how that impacts on their behaviours and states of mind.

Our unconscious mind:
- Works with patterns and symbols to shorten the learning process and enable us to respond quickly and automatically to various triggers.
- Is home to our memories and how we store our memories so that we can recall them easily and accurately.
- Automatically generates emotions like fear and anger based on our fight or flight response.
- Creates and maintains our habits and how we develop problematic behaviour and thinking.
- Is in charge of our ability to learn and learns through repetition.
- Takes the path of least resistance to enable us to progress and grow. This sometimes results in laziness and taking shortcuts.
- Represses negative emotions that we haven't dealt with properly and represents them to us for resolution, sometimes when we least need them!
- Runs our body and is in charge of our health and healing.
- Helps us to create our own unique model of the world based on our perceptions of reality.
- Listens to and responds to our conscious thoughts and instructions.

Giving the unconscious mind the right type of instruction is fundamental to effective mind management.

CHAPTER 5

Communicating

It is easy to think of communication as something that just takes place between you and other people, and we know now that it is so much more than that.

Your communication starts internally and results in your behaviour. People are not their behaviours. Whatever you see as resulting behaviour in someone else, is not the essence of who they are, it is as a result of how they are communicating within.

A child throws his dummy out of the pram. "You are a bad boy," his mother scolds him. This is not true, he is so much more than that, obviously, but his behaviour at that time may not have been acceptable or desirable to the mother.

Later in the day the mother and her child are resting in the park watching some older boys playing. A fight breaks out between the older boys "Bad boys do bad things." She indicates to the child. The child's unconscious mind refers back to the earlier statement and the child learns, "I am a bad boy. Bad boys do bad things. That is me, that is what I do."

It is so easy for communication to get mixed up. **You are not your behaviour and you are not the way that you are feeling**. If you are feeling low, if you are feeling stressed, if you are angry, depressed, frustrated, anxious or sad, then this is just the result of the way that you are thinking at the moment. It isn't permanent, it can be changed, it is not the only way that you behave and it is not all that you are.

A child that is behaving badly can, at the next moment be immensely loving and generous. We all have the potential to behave badly, we all have the potential to feel depressed, stressed and sad. We all have the potential to be loving and generous towards other people and feel happy and joyous. Even mass murderers have this potential.

If you are not getting the results that you want in life, then do not accept that "this is just the way that things are." Realise now that human beings are built to change, to adapt. Your mind is an amazing piece of equipment, you are the captain of your ship and your mind will respond to your commands. You can change and if you want to change, then you will change. You *can* get the results that you want in life.

Our Internal Communication Process

Let us have a look at how this process of internal communication works and how we construct our model of the world to give us our reality.

We experience our world through our senses. Senses of sight, hearing, taste, smell and touch. We collect data from the outside world via our eyes, ears, nose, mouth and skin and we translate this data or these bits of information into our reality. We are talking about a lot of bits. According to the Encyclopedia Britannica we are exposed to around eleven million bits of information every second, with the eyes responsible for taking in ten million of those bits.

Somehow our brain needs to interpret these bits of information for us so that we can understand them and make sense of them. This is the function that is performed by our unconscious mind.

Internal Representations

In the processing of the data our unconscious mind prioritises and deletes bits, it uses our memories to decide what is important. It compares the information coming in to the data stored in our system and it spots patterns, things that we have experienced before. It reviews the commands that it has previously received from our conscious mind, like the decisions that we have made and it produces an internal representation. The internal representations are what we experience consciously and make up our present moment experience. They also form our memories.

In any moment in time when we have our eyes open we will be seeing things, hearing things, tasting things, smelling things, and touching things. We will not always be consciously aware that we are doing all of these things. What are you touching and smelling at the moment? What are you hearing? Were you aware that you were experiencing this before I asked you to think about it? In any one moment we have the opportunity to experience all of these things but we tend to concentrate on only what seems important at the time. In your case you are concentrating on reading and using your visual sense and you may not have been consciously aware of what you are touching with your legs. When you think about it though, you are able to gain a representation of what your legs are touching and whether it is hard or soft, the air around your legs, the fabric of your clothes. When you think back later in the day you will probably be able to recall parts of the experience of this moment and remember bits of the representations that you have now.

We unconsciously generate representations of things that we are seeing, hearing, tasting, smelling and touching now, things that represent the external world now. We are also able to call up representations from our unconscious mind from our stored memories. We are able to make pictures in our minds eye, we are able to recall sounds, how things feel, how things made us feel, tastes and smells. These are part of our created internal world.

If you have not thought before about the fact that you are able to create pictures internally from memories, then go and stand in front of the mirror, look at a particular part of your body, then close your eyes and remember what you saw. Were you able to bring back the picture?

Think about a piece of fruit, an apple say. Close your eyes and see yourself holding a nice big juicy apple in your hand. Do that now.

How detailed were the pictures that you saw? What could you pick out? Could you also feel how heavy the apple is, could you imagine how it would smell? We are all able to make pictures, some of us a more detailed picture than others, and this is a skill that we can develop.

A state of mind

The sum total of our internal representations at any one moment in time lead to our state of mind.

If what we are experiencing is agreeable to us, then we may be in a positive state of mind. If we are experiencing negative thoughts then we may describe our state of mind as unhappy or negative. Common states of mind include: happy, motivated, confused, confident, sad, fearful, powerful, stuck, calm, angry, focussed, loved, energetic.

Bear in mind that our internal representations are made up of our unconscious mind's interpretation of events in the outside world and also thoughts that we are creating internally.

We could be walking down a quiet country lane on a beautiful sunny, warm afternoon, hand in hand with a loved one, and at the same time we could be in a very anxious state of mind. How can that happen? Well, at the same time as experiencing all the beauty of the world around us and some great company we also could be thinking about all of the things that have gone wrong in our life recently, and all of the things that could potentially go wrong for us in the future. It is also possible that we may judge walking as being a negative experience. We may not like quiet country lanes, we may prefer cooler days and we may prefer to be alone. In fact, we may prefer to be sitting with our feet up at home on the sofa and if we are thinking about this then we may be resenting what we are doing in the moment.

Likewise if we are carrying negative emotions around from previous arguments or events, we may be feeling these emotions whilst we are on our walk and this will affect our state of mind.

Bear in mind that our state of mind is changing constantly as we experience different things and think different thoughts. A succession of negative thoughts can put us in the doldrums, however our mood can change in an instant if we get distracted by something that happens and we judge that thing to be really positive. We could be on our walk, feeling really anxious, thinking about the hundred and one things that we have to do later in the day when all of a sudden we see a Kingfisher dive into the river by the side of the lane. This one thing can take over our entire thinking, all of our attention moves towards the Kingfisher, our negative thoughts are lost as we absorb the events of the moment. We experience delight at seeing this natural wonder and the beauty of the bird. Our mood lifts instantly.

Our physiology

You can often read many things about another person's thinking and state of mind from just watching them. How do you judge that someone is feeling happy or sad, angry or calm? If you watch the way that they are standing or sitting you may get a clue. Are they sitting upright or slumped in the chair? You can observe their facial expressions. Are they smiling or grimacing? Is their face flushed? Are they gritting their teeth or is their jaw relaxed? Are their eyes wide open with pupils dilated or squinting?

Pretty much all of these cues are unconscious on the part of the other person and happen as a result of how they are experiencing the world at that moment in time. Are their internal representations positive for them or negative? What is their state of mind?

We can't help but communicate via our physiology because our body is dynamically linked to our thinking by the unconscious mind. Deeper inside the body other changes are constantly taking place, our blood pressure changes, our breathing changes, our heart beats faster, our body becomes warmer and cooler depending on what we are thinking about and concentrating on. Our energy levels are determined by the food that we put into our bodies and also what we are experiencing in life.

If you are excited by a task that you are doing, then your heart beats faster, your body warms up, your breathing accelerates, you feel energised. These are deeply unconscious reactions and they form part of our structure of internal communication.

Behaviour

We demonstrate our thoughts using hand and arm signals. Some of us do this more than most. If someone is frantically moving their arms around as they are talking we may describe them as talking animatedly. This would imply that there is a fair amount of energy going into the communication, they may be excited, annoyed, or struggling to get their point across but they certainly are not calm.

Our tone of voice, the speed of our speech, the resonance and the quality of our voice will often provide an indication of the thoughts that we are processing. If we are angry, we raise our voice, we speak more quickly, sometimes our voice wobbles with the emotion. All of this normally takes place unconsciously.

More obviously, we make conscious decisions based on the information that the unconscious mind provides us. We decide which words to use, what to say, we decide what actions to take in every given situation and this is all dependent on the representations that we have that make up what we see, hear, feel, taste and smell and the internal thoughts that we are having.

It is Monday morning. I am feeling overwhelmed with the amount of work that I have to do. There are just so many things that are tearing at my attention. I have a deadline of midday for a piece of work that needs to be completed and sent to my boss. Over the weekend a number of emails have come in from other members of staff that need my attention, and they all want a reply straight away. My computer is playing up and running really slowly, so I need to get the IT people to have a look at it but that will have to wait. I have had a great weekend, really relaxing. I would rather still be at home with my feet up. The washer broke at the weekend and I need to get in touch with a plumber to come out to have a look at it. I have been trying to get through to the manufacturers by phone and I have spent half an hour in a queue, I gave up. Just so many things to do.

My boss pops her head around the door to my office, and she is not smiling. "Have you got a minute?" She proceeds to hand over another half a dozen tasks for me to do.

Are you kidding me? You must be having a laugh. I haven't got time for all of that.

I smile begrudgingly at her as she leaves me to my misery.

Two minutes later a junior member of staff knocks on the open door to my office and walks straight in. "Sorry to interrupt. I just wondered if you would mind if I took a couple of hours off this morning? It's just that my daughter's hamster is not very well and

I need to take it to the vets"

You can imagine that at this stage my behaviour may not necessarily be the best for fostering great staff relations! I may well react poorly and say something that I later regret. The request may well be completely reasonable, in fact the member of staff may be really upset and my reaction to them might make it worse. Even if I reply politely and grant their request the chances are that they will recognise that something was not totally sitting right with me, because I can't hind my physiological response.

This illustrates how easy it is for us to create unwanted behaviour and communication breakdowns. My state of mind is determined by the thoughts that I am having, "I am overwhelmed by the amount of work that I have to do." I am wishing that it was still the weekend. External events take place that makes my mood worse: I can't get through on the phone to the washing machine manufacturers, my computer is slow, my boss gives me more work to do - all these internal representations are interpreted by me as being negative and increase the feeling of overwhelm and agitation.

The way that we filter the information in our mind which we receive through our senses will often determine how we experience events, it will form our memories and it will determine our actions and behaviour.

Mind Filtering Unit

There are eleven million bits of information per second coming into our brain via our senses, too many for us to handle in our awareness. Our unconscious mind performs the duty of filtering those bits of information for us to make them understandable, manageable and so that we can act and react. As a processing unit our brain can only handle a very small proportion of these bits, something like 50 bits and so we lose a vast quantity of information before it reaches our conscious awareness through this filtering process.

In fact, according to psychologist George Miller's paper "The Magical Number Seven, Plus or Minus Two" (1956), we can only store seven plus or minus two chunks of information per second in our conscious memory. That is not five to nine *bits* of information, but between five and nine separate *chunks* of information which may be made up of several bits.

The chunks of information that we are aware of consist of our internal representations. We receive a representation of our world based on the filtering that takes place in the unconscious mind. We unconsciously delete, distort and generalise information to get the number of bits down from eleven million to the 50 that we can handle consciously.

Interestingly, we each delete, distort and generalise in slightly different ways because our mind filters are determined by our unique beliefs, decisions, memories, values and attitudes. In this way we each have our own model of the world.

Deletion

Think now about how your left thumb feels at this moment. Where was that feeling before I mentioned it? In every moment in time we have the potential to be aware of sights, sounds, tastes, smells, touch and feelings from all over the body. We delete some of this information, just as you had deleted the feeling in your left thumb until we brought it into conscious awareness. We delete information so that we can concentrate on what we perceive to be important.

Have you ever lost your car keys? You can't find them anywhere and then you notice them on the kitchen worktop, they had been in front of you all the time. Have you ever experienced anything like that? That is deletion. The chances are that you have been panicking about being late and all of your chunks of information at that time have been used up, so your brain deletes various things. This is also how sometimes you end up forgetting your phone, your umbrella.

You are sitting at the table reading a book or reading something on your tablet computer. You are so deeply engrossed that you do not even notice when someone asks you a question. Selective attention is also deletion.

Distortion

People who worked with Steve Jobs, former CEO at Apple, used to say that he lived through his own "reality distortion field." He distorted reality to make it fit his model of the world. Steve's team would tell him that things could not be done the way that he wanted them. He would make them believe that somehow it was possible, and they would find a way. They then went ahead and made it possible. By this means he was responsible for the ideas and for the production of technology that people had previously thought was impossible.

In our own way, we are all able to dream, fantasize and distort reality. Our distortions can assist us or they can hinder us. We create fears that we think are real and that end up limiting our lives: I'm not good enough, I don't have the ability to do such and such. We distort through the assumptions that we make over the way that people perceive us. "They think that I am too introverted to make a good manager."

Much of our great art, literature and music is created using distortion. Think of Salvador Dali, he used distortion in his own thoughts to create many of his master pieces and he encourages distortion in the minds of people appreciating his art. The more attention that you pay to his paintings, the more that you begin to see.

When I was a teenager we lived in a house with a very creaky central heating system. Occasionally I would be at home alone and the noises from the central heating system used to play tricks with my mind. I know now that the creaks came from the heating up and cooling down of pipes in the system as water flowed through them. At the time I heard the noises and I wondered if there was someone in the house, treading on the creaky floorboards. The more I heard the creaks, the more convinced I became that there was someone there. I imagined whereabouts in the house they were. I could hear them coming up the stairs closer to me, I lay in bed terrified. Nobody was ever there.

Sometimes when I am out running in the countryside I see shapes in the distance. Generally they are shapes made by bushes and trees but it is possible to see them as shapes of animals. The more that I concentrate on them the more I can imagine that they are animals. I have my own distortion field and so do you.

Generalisation

Another tactic that we have for reducing the amount of information that we are dealing with is to generalise. We notice patterns, principles and rules in everything, the unconscious mind is programmed to work with symbols and to chunk information together. We are able to recognise classes of objects such as telephones, tablet computers and trees even though individual objects have their own unique physical structure. We use words to generalise and categorise.

New behaviour that we observe in other people and behaviour that we carry out ourselves is made up of bits and pieces of behaviour that we have previously seen or experienced. We are able to generalise using our experience to allow us to replicate or label the behaviour so that we do not have to figure out how to do it from scratch. This saves lots of time and energy in constantly learning new behaviours.

Sometimes we become limited by our own generalisations. If you have ever experienced learning a subject as being difficult for you, then there is a danger that you may perceive all future learning opportunities as being difficult. You may decide to do something familiar to you instead of learning new things. This may be one reason why some people become less curious as they get older, they generalise that they have seen it all before.

Normally we do not just filter our experience using either deletion, distortion or generalisation, we do each of these things together. When I mistake the shape of a bush for an animal I am deleting certain bits of information that would lead me to realise that it is in fact a bush, I am distorting my perception and I am generalising the perception as recognising parts of an animal in the shape and apparent colour of the bush.

Projecting perceptions

Have you ever met someone for the first time and thought that they remind you of someone else? It happens all the time and now we know why.

We pick up signals through the way that someone looks, behaves, talks and they remind us of someone else. Our unconscious mind recognises some patterns in what we see in the person and it trawls through our memory bank to find matching characteristics in someone that we know. It then picks out this person as being similar.

Let us assume that we meet Geoff for the first time just before we go into a meeting with him. He greets us with a big smile and seems very pleased to meet us. As he talks, Geoff reminds us of someone that we used to work with called John. We are not sure what it is that reminds us of him - it is just a feeling.

Now John was a real pain in the neck, he was really argumentative and we did not really ever see eye to eye with him. How do you think that we are going to be feeling going into the meeting with Geoff?

Once we have made that association between the two people then we may encounter some deletion, distortion and generalisation in our thinking as we communicate with Geoff and as the information that is coming to us passes through our mind filtering unit. We will find that we associate the decisions and beliefs that we had of John with Geoff. Geoff did not do anything wrong but he never stands a chance with us, poor fellow.

Over time, as we get to know him, Geoff will make his own unique impact on us and we will start to form beliefs and decisions about him that reflect the way that we experience him. But this may take some time.

Whenever we observe someone we give them a certain personality, certain characteristics, we think that they look a certain way, they have certain characteristics according to our observation and according to our personal filters. The thing is that in order to recognise those characteristics we must be familiar with them. In order to recognise anger in another person we must have some experience of anger ourselves. If we see someone as being mean, then in order to recognise this we must have experienced what it is like to be mean to other people.

Let us assume that you are on a train reading a book and next to you there is a father and his two young sons. The father is staring out of the window whilst his sons are creating mayhem, shouting and throwing things at each other. As the journey continues so the children's behaviour gets worse. The father seems oblivious to his sons' actions and continues to look out of the window. You are finding it impossible to concentrate on your book.

As this drama takes place you start to make assumptions and give the father certain labels in your mind. Neglectful, disrespectful to others, uncaring. If the family get up and leave the train at the next stop then that will be your lasting impression of him. You decide to challenge the father.

"Excuse me. Is there any chance that you could ask your children to quieten down a bit?"

"I'm so sorry." Says the father. "We have just left the hospital where my wife is in intensive care. I was miles away."

You are not your behaviour and other people are not their behaviour. You perceive other people through your own filters. Your beliefs about people are not facts. They are true to you at the time but they are not fact in the world. You project your own negative and positive emotions onto other people and believe that they are true.

Whenever you are carrying around emotional baggage then you will increasingly notice these same emotions in other people. If you are experiencing a period of significant anger in your life, then you will particularly pay attention to what you perceive as anger in other people. This is one of the reasons for the saying "trouble attracts trouble."

If other people's behaviour is causing you problems in your life then it will help you to think of this and realise that whatever you are thinking of that other person is actually your own projection, it is not them. You have the power to change your perceptions and the first stage in doing this is to become aware of them.

Key Points

- We have choices over how we interpret events and how we think.
- We create our states of mind and our moods.
- It is our judgement of events and circumstances that determines whether they are good or bad for us.
- We each have a mind filtering system that we use to process information that we take in through our senses. We unconsciously delete, distort and generalise the millions of bits of information that we receive every second. This ensures that

we do not become continuously overloaded with information and this leaves us with our representation of reality.
- The main downside of the mind filtering that takes place is that sometimes we delete and distort information in such a way that it distorts our reality. This is often the reason for unwanted habits and behaviours. This mind filtering system is partly responsible for the way that we feel, for how we manage stress, for how we perceive others, and it is within our domain of influence. We can change our perceptions and change our reality.

CHAPTER 6

Your power to change

You are amazing. You are unique. Your mind and body are built to support you in growing and developing throughout your life, even well into old age. We are all born with the potential to achieve whatever we put our minds to during our lifetime.

It was once thought that we were born with a certain number of brain cells, neurons, and that these brain cells gradually died over our lifetime, never to be replaced. We now know that not to be true. We are constantly developing new brain cells throughout adult life through a process called neurogenesis. In fact our brain actually changes shape according to how we use it, what demands we place on it and what skills we develop. This is called neuro-plasticity.

So, if you think that you can't change, or you are too old to change, then think again. **You will change and you are changing constantly, throughout life**. Every decision that you make or don't make changes your life in some way. Your decision to read this book changed your life because you have spent time reading this rather than doing something else. The ideas that you are reading have changed you already in some way.

Oliver Wendell Holmes said "A mind stretched to a new idea never regains its original shape." He was right!

You have choices in life, you can do the same things and create the same results, or you can make better decisions and get better results.

In some ways we are conditioned by society into thinking that we can blame other people and other things for our problems and our lack of ability to influence our lives. Myths are established that support us in passing over responsibility for our results. People say "I am too old to change now." This is not true, it is a myth and it gives people an excuse to avoid the perceived pain in doing something new.

When I was at school an English teacher there told my class that there was nobody in the class that had the ability to write a book. He essentially said "you are not good enough". We hear this sort of thing all the time and it sinks in unconsciously so that whenever we consider the possibility of doing something we think, *I can't do that because I am not good enough.* That one statement by that teacher gave everyone in the class an excuse not to write a book.

Jessica Ennis-Hill, won a gold medal at the London Olympics in the Heptathlon. She says in her autobiography that she was told throughout her career that she was "too small" to be any good in her field. She had the excuses if she wanted to take them but she chose otherwise and so can you.

Whenever you ask someone to do something for you they will either do it or they will give you a bunch of reasons why they could not do it. Whatever people think their reasons are, they are not reasons, they are essentially excuses. They will blame the weather, the traffic, the economy, their partners, their family. Anything rather than taking responsibility for their own results. People will even blame their own shortcomings rather than decide to do something about them. "I'm not very good at following instructions." They say it as if it is a fact and they cannot do anything about it.

In any situation **you can choose** to take **responsibility** or make excuses. You can choose to be the cause of your own success, or you can be at the effect of other people and things. You can change now by choosing to take responsibility in all areas of your life including your thinking. This does not take time, this is a change that you can make now.

Neuroplasticity

You know, if we want to change the results that we are getting in life, then we have been given all the tools to enable us to do that. We just need to get smart about understanding the tools that we have and how to use them in pursuit of our goals.

Fields of neuroscience and genetics have developed rapidly over recent years. Until quite recently it was thought that neurons only existed in the brain. It is now recognised that they exist throughout the entire nervous system. Until around the 1970s, an accepted idea across neuroscience was that the nervous system was essentially fixed throughout adulthood. A relatively new concept in neuroscience has emerged called neuroplasticity.

Neuroplasticity or brain plasticity refers to the now acknowledged characteristics of the brain and nervous system being moldable and changeable in structure, changing throughout life in response to changes in behaviour, environmental changes and thought processes.

In a 2009 study, scientists made two groups of mice swim a water maze, and then in a separate trial subjected them to an unpleasant stimulus to see how quickly they would learn to move away from it. Then, over the next four weeks they allowed one group of mice to run inside their rodent wheels, an activity most mice enjoy. Meanwhile they forced the other group to work harder on mini treadmills at a speed and duration controlled by the scientists.

They then tested both groups again to track their learning skills and memory. Both groups of mice improved their performances in the water maze from the earlier trial. But only the extra-worked treadmill runners were better in the avoidance task, a skill that, according to neuroscientists, demands a more complicated cognitive response.

The mice who were forced to run on the treadmills showed evidence of molecular changes in several portions of their brains when viewed under a microscope, while the voluntary wheel-runners had changes in only one area. Chauying J. Jen, a professor of physiology and an author of the study, said. "Our results support the notion that different forms of exercise induce neuroplasticity changes in different brain regions,"

By changing the way that you train, the training that you take, the way that you exercise, the way that you stimulate the body and brain, you can improve your results.

So, if you can change the shape of your brain by deliberate use of the body, how about the other way round?

Hypnosis allows communication directly with the unconscious mind. By distracting and subduing the conscious mind with an involving story or a point of focus the hypnotist is able to get access to the powerful resources of the unconscious mind. In an experiment at a Psychology Department in a London hospital, a woman was prepared to be hypnotised. The woman was shown several hot pokers that were in the room. The hypnotist proceeded to hypnotise her and once he judged that she was sufficiently relaxed he touched her arm with his fingers and said quietly, "I am placing a red hot poker on your arm" She flinched with pain and immediately a red weal appeared on her arm where the hypnotist had touched her.

Imagine you are in the kitchen. You take a fresh red apple from the fruit bowl. It is cool in your hand. The skin feels smooth and waxy. At one end there is a small wooden stalk growing out of a small basin. The apple is shiny, firm and quite heavy for its size as you look at it in the palm of your hand.

You raise the apple to your nose. It gives off such a characteristic, unmistakable sweet apply smell doesn't it? You take a sharp knife and cut the apple in half. The two halves fall apart, the red shiny outer skin contrasting with the drops of translucent apple juice that gently ooze out. The apple smell is now slightly stronger.

Now you bite deeply into the apple and let the juice swirl around your mouth. That sweet red apple flavour is unmistakable. Stop a second! Is your mouth watering? Is your stomach rumbling? It is possible to see, feel and taste the apple as if you are actually experiencing eating it. The implications of this are fascinating, nothing actually happened. It was all in your imagination and your unconscious mind cannot distinguish between what is real and what you are imagining and thus your salivary glands were stimulated to wash away the sweet taste.

These are skills that we can build up over time. We can create pictures, sounds, feelings. Fortunately we can usually easily use our conscious mind to distinguish between what is going on in the outside world and what we do on the inside. Also, when we store these pictures, sounds and feelings in our memory we can distinguish between what actually happened and what we imagined or created internally.

Have you ever had time away from a loved one and imagined hugging them and as a result you felt your heart racing? Then you will understand that at least part of you thought that the image and feelings of hugging someone were actually real.

If you have ever woken up in the middle of a bad dream, then you may remember the feelings, the emotion, and the way that your body responded to those feelings and emotions, you may even have been sweating, or shaking. In order for you to experience that some part of your brain must have communicated to your body that this is a real experience and you need to react. The fact that as human beings we have the ability to create thoughts in our head and for our bodies to respond provides us with amazing potential to influence our future.

Here is an example from the cancer counselling and research centre in Dallas Texas. Dr Simmonton who was the medical director there was treating a patient who was diagnosed with a fatal form of throat cancer. The patient was told that he had less that a five percent chance of surviving, he lost thirty percent of his body weight and was extremely weak, could hardly swallow and was having trouble breathing. In fact his own medical doctors were debating whether to give him any treatment at all, because they believed that it would probably only add to his discomfort without actually increasing his chances of surviving.

Dr Simmonton though taught this patient some mental imagery and relaxation techniques that he had been working on. As he was receiving the radiation treatment three times per day, this patient pictured millions of tiny bullets of energy bombarding his cells. He also visualised the cancer cells as weaker than his normal cells so that when they received the radiation treatment they were unable to repair the damage that they suffered. He visualised his body's white blood cells as the soldiers of the immune system, coming in and swarming all over the dead and dying cancer cells and then carrying them to his liver and kidneys to be flushed right out of his body.

The results from this treatment and his visualisation were amazing. He suffered hardly any of the side effects of that sort of treatment. He put his weight back on and in two months all signs of his cancer had totally vanished. Dr Simmonton was so amazed by this and encouraged by it that he taught this visualisation technique to other patients with what was perceived to be incurable cancer. The average survival time of this group of patients was more than double the expected life span of somebody with that type of cancer.

Neurons and neurotransmitters

How can all of this work? Well it's all down to the process of communication that we have going on in our bodies, the process of communication that is carried out by our neurons, our cells and our neurotransmitters.

The neuron used to be known to as a brain cell, a cell specifically located in the brain. But now we recognise that neurons exist throughout the nervous system, so a better description is a nerve cell.

Neurons consist basically of an axon, which is the body of the neuron and dendrites which are like tentacles that stretch away from the neurons towards the dendrites of other cells. Each neuron can have many dendrites. Neurons carry the messages that we send through our thoughts, experiences and actions to other neurons in our body via a communication process that involves billions of connections. They carry the messages as electrical pulses through the axon until they reach the end of the dendrites at which stage they convert to a chemical process. Things called neurotransmitters are produced from the dendrites. These are the chemicals that transfer the messages from neuron to neuron.

You may be familiar with the names of some of our neurotransmitters: dopamine, serotonin, adrenaline, glutamate, endorphins. Addictive drugs usually have an effect on our dopamine system, **as does exercise**. Seratonin is linked to our feelings of happiness and well-being. This system can also be positively affected by exercise, thus the term "an exercise high". The positive impact of exercise cannot be understated. The release of these positive neurotransmitters can also be stimulated by meditation and Mindfulness.

Neurotransmitters carry signals across a gap between the neurons called a synaptic gap. Once they reach the dendrites of a neighbouring neuron they convert to an electrical pulse again as the process continues.
When I say that there are billions of these connections in the body

I mean BILLIONS. The average adult is estimated to have 100 billion neurons and each one of these neurons has on average 7,000 synaptic connections to other neurons.

Endocrinologist and Author, Deepak Chopra said that "every cell in your body is eavesdropping on your thoughts."

When we keep saying to ourselves "I am stressed" and "I have no energy", just imagine the process of electrical and chemical communication that takes place throughout our body. Is it any surprise then that eventually we feel really stressed or tired?

By adjusting your thinking, your food and drink intake, your actions, by watching out for your internal saboteur you have the power to change now.

Key Points

- Through a process of neurogenesis and neuroplasticity we learn that our minds change throughout our lifetime. We can do the same things and create the same results, or we can make better decisions and get better results.
- We continue to produce brain cells throughout life and these cells communicate with each other to carry our thoughts throughout our bodies.
- There is a chemical processes involved in the transmission of energy throughout our body. It determines how our actions and what we put into our bodies affect how we feel, our level of happiness and our sense of well-being.

CHAPTER 7

Our Inner Saboteur

One of the consequences of our fight or flight response is that we are constantly on the look out for anything that we consider may cause us pain. From the time in our evolution when we were being chased by wild animals we have inherited a fear mechanism that is related to the possibility of pain.

Whenever we encounter a situation where we see the possibility of pain we automatically trigger our fear response and we back off. As we now know, the unconscious mind cannot distinguish between what is real and what is imagined, so we can actually trigger the fear response just by thinking about a situation where we may encounter pain.

We are not just talking about physical pain. We also trigger the fear response by thinking about emotional pain: hurt, sadness. Emotional pain or psychological pain includes forms of mental suffering, mental torment.

This type of fear can be **the single most destructive thing to you achieving your potential** and it is a fear that is spread and reinforced by society, your friends and your family. It builds in every one of us an inner saboteur that sits there waiting to limit our lives and sabotage our chances of success.

When you are growing up you are curious, you are excited by what you can achieve in life. You are enthusiastic and you start dreaming of all the possibilities that life holds for you, what you want to become, what you want to do……

……and then you get talked out of it. People gradually pour water on your fire for life and they put it out.

People will tell you that you are "not good enough" to do what you want to do. Why do they do that? Because they do not want you to get disappointed when some way down the line you fail. They do not want you to get hurt. Hurt equals psychological pain. Fight or flight response.

We get told not to aim too high as we will get hurt in the fall. We learn that we are too tall, too small, too clever, too active, too poor to achieve our dreams, people do not want us to suffer emotional pain associated with failure.

We get warned not to stand out from the crowd for fear of looking stupid. That is, in their eyes we might make them look stupid, and also we might make a fool of ourselves. This is fear of mental suffering.

All of these messages lead to us setting up an inner sabotage mechanism. They tell us that we can not have what we want in life. They tell us that if there is the potential for psychological pain then we need to avoid that at all costs. **Our inner saboteur is born**.

Our inner saboteur lives in our unconscious mind. It abides by the rules of the unconscious mind; so it learns by repetition, it looks for similarities, patterns and it is habitual. All of these messages that we receive from well meaning people in our youth reinforce the strength of our saboteur and they teach it to play a prominent part in our thinking. Whenever we are "in danger" of getting what we want in life, whenever we have a chance to make life better, our inner saboteur gets triggered and comes out to play.

Decisions

We hear people say, "I am my own worst enemy." This is the saboteur in action. We are constantly offered opportunities to make decisions that can make a positive difference to our lives. We have an opportunity for change and we have a decision to make, *do we decide to change or stay the same?*

We consider the options, *change may be better in the long run, but what happens if....?* We get a feeling of discomfort, it may appear as mild anxiety and something inside tells us to just leave things as they are. *Better the devil that you know.* We decide to stay the same. We have been persuaded by our inner saboteur.

Back in the day of Christopher Columbus most sailors would not dare to lose sight of land on their voyages. Stories of fatalities at sea abounded. They would set sail and travel parallel to the safety of land. Columbus had other ideas, he set off at ninety degrees to land, straight out into the ocean. At some stage his saboteur must have come out and said *What on earth are you doing? What about the risks?* He was able to overcome his saboteur and his fear, he did it anyway and the world has never been the same since.

History is littered with stories of people overcoming their psychological fears. In the minds of these people the potential reward outweighs the risk and potential pain of failure. They recognise the potential for pain but they go ahead and do it anyway. These are the people who change the world.

It is easy to think of superstars, celebrities, pioneers, leaders, explorers as being cut from a different cloth to us. We consider them lucky to have their talents, their opportunities, their confidence. The thing is that in reality they experience the same doubts, the same fears, they have a saboteur inside, just as you and I do. We enjoy watching stars rise and somehow we experience a certain satisfaction in seeing their occasional meltdown. We realise that they are just like us.

Steve Jobs was adopted as a young child. He grew up in humble surroundings, his parents made sacrifices to give him a comfortable home and they encouraged him to indulge in his passions. He started Apple Inc. from the garage in his parents' home with a few friends.

Later in life, in a rare interview Steve explained his epiphany. He said that the world teaches us to have a nice life, get a job, to fit in and coast along quietly making no noise. He said that **everything changed** for him the day that he realised that everything in the world was created by "someone no smarter than you." This became a decision in his life that propelled him to change the shape of technology in the world for ever.

When Apple launched the iPad people said that it would fail, customers would not like it, would not use it. Other technology companies had toyed with the idea of launching a tablet computer but they had decided that it could not be done and would not work. Their saboteurs recognised the potential for pain, this prompted them to scrap the idea. Steve Jobs constantly came across people who told him that he would fail, that his ideas were crazy and that they would never become reality. He managed his saboteur and decided differently.

Comfort Zone

Whenever we think about doing something new, exposing ourselves to new ideas, taking on learning, we take a risk. We venture out into the unknown. We are conditioned to think of risk as the potential for pain and this triggers our saboteur, our reptilian brain and we feel some kind of resistance to it inside.

Behind all resistance to something new is fear, but there is never anything to fear. The unknown is where possibility lies. Pain and adversity are powerful vehicles to promote personal growth. We come to see pain as a negative experience. This is judgement and a false belief and behind it is pure fear. Life is made up of seasons and painful times do not last, on the other side of pain and your fear is your potential.

We want to fit in, we want to be part of the clan, we want people to love us and we are afraid to stand out. This is nothing more than being imprisoned by our fears. Developing courage is not to live in the absence of fear. It is the willingness to acknowledge our fears and walk through them in pursuit of goals that are important to us.

Think of the stories of some prisoners who would rather stay in jail than be faced with release from prison. They get used to the routines and perceived safety of prison life. On the day of their release from prison, faced with a lack of routine, change and the unknown the overriding emotion that these prisoners feel is fear. To the extent that some of them go out and immediately commit a minor crime in order to be sent back to prison and back to the comfort of their routines, they return to their comfort zone. They sabotage their chances of a better existence in favour of returning to what is familiar to them.

It is important for you to get to know your saboteur and to get to understand your own comfort zone. The comfort zone is something that some people spend their whole lives living in. In this zone life is comfortable. It is comfortable because you know it, and whatever you know becomes comfortable. People follow the same routines day after day, year after year because then they know what outcomes to expect.

We make decisions on our future based on what feels best to us and very often something that is familiar will feel better than something that is unknown to us. This is a typical example of our saboteur at work. As we go through life we reject opportunities to change and opportunities to explore alternatives, opportunities to grow because they do not feel as comfortable to us as that which is familiar. So we stay the same. In this way we create our comfort zones.

Life in the comfort zone is fairly good. It is very rarely really good and very rarely really bad. Things just get quite bad and quite good before they return to normal.

When you ask someone how they are, what do they say? "I'm okay." "Not bad." "Been better, been worse."

People are so afraid of things not being okay that they settle for okay. "How's it going today?" "Not bad," they say. For some people it never gets any better than that. It is as though there is something stopping them from saying "Everything is great thanks. I'm doing fantastic." That something is fear, it is their saboteur.

We fall into the trap of waiting for good things to come along to get us out of our comfort zone and make life a little bit better for us. People say, "I'll be better once the weekend is here." "I'll be better once the sun comes out." We pass over responsibility for our happiness to outside influences and in this way we give away our power to other things and other people. This is also our saboteur at work.

When you say "How are things with you?" And people reply, "Not bad." They wish it could be better, but they are so afraid of it being bad that they do not do anything. They hope that their life will magically change and that it will stay the same at the same time. We hear people say, "It could be worse." This is pure fear and it is stopping people from developing and realising their dreams. It is trapping them in their comfort zone.

Sometimes opportunities come along that are too good to turn down, although we do our best to make excuses to stay the same. On these occasions we are forced out of our comfort zone, and it does not feel great at first, in fact it feels really uncomfortable. We feel out of our depth, we suffer confusion, we are overwhelmed and we wish we could go back to the way that we were. These are the periods where we are growing. We think that we are in pain and we long for the pain to be over and for things to begin to feel normal again, normal and comfortable. We look for opportunities to retreat quietly to our comfort zone without "losing face." The thing is that on the other side of our pain is our destiny.

We are occasionally forced out of our comfort zone by "bad things" happening to us. Sometimes we are forced to change. It could be a health scare, it could be redundancy, it could be the ending of a relationship. Again we are put in a place that feels uncomfortable, we feel pain and then gradually we start recreating our happiness. Sometimes life can even get better.

The only way to create a better life is to undergo change. Make decisions that take you outside of your comfort zone. If you are not experiencing a little bit of discomfort on a daily basis then you are not growing.

You are reading this for a reason, you are not reading it by accident. There may be some things that you are reading that are making you feel a bit uncomfortable. You are being asked to think in a slightly different way, a way that may be pushing you outside of your comfort zone. At least, I hope so because that way you are going to be growing.

Twice in my life I became the top sales person in my roles at the time. Each time when I achieved top position I looked for a new challenge. Each time I changed job. On both occasions people told me that I was crazy to give up what I had built. I did not look at it as giving up what I had, I looked at it as moving forward and growing into a new challenge. Did my saboteur come out and play? Yes, I had my doubts and I underwent a period of uncertainty and discomfort as I learned new things, met new people and experienced new challenges. Each time I pushed the boundaries of my comfort zone and I believe that I grew in character and certainly grew new skills.

When I left employment for good and set up my own training and coaching business, again people questioned with me whether I knew what I was doing? Would I make a success of it? What about giving up all of the benefits of employment like security of income and a pension? My saboteur certainly made an appearance over this decision as I stared out into my future and looked at all of the unknowns. I can't say that starting my own business was without pain, there was a period of time when I had no income at all. Every time I looked at my finances my saboteur came out and I felt fearful of running out of money. I counted the months until I would need to start employment again. I worked hard, I applied my skills. I built new skills and I started earning an income again. I started concentrating on what I needed to do to make a success out of my business rather than what could go wrong and my feelings of fear receded. I subdued my saboteur and it was satisfied.

I am constantly looking for ways of growing. I know that I need to step outside of my comfort zone in order to do that and I challenge myself to feel the fear, almost enjoy it and move forward.

Please note: I am not encouraging wanton risk taking. You should always make a study of possible consequences before you act. Consider the consequences for you, for the people around you and for the planet. Realise when you are feeling fear, recognise that it is your saboteur, your reptilian brain and make a decision with all of the information available to you. Moving jobs is not always the answer, leaving relationships is not always the answer. Pushing yourself to be the best that you can be where you are right now may be the answer for you. You create more opportunities for yourself when you are the best in the business at what you do.

Whatever you do, challenge your boundaries, because your boundaries are likely to be self imposed. Roger Bannister was the first person to run a mile in under four minutes. It had become known as the "four minute mile barrier". Roger broke down the barrier first in his own mind and then on the track. Within a short period of time many more athletes also ran the mile in under four minutes. There was no discovery of new running techniques. The equipment had not changed. The only thing that had changed was the world's perception of what was possible.

Key Points

- We each have an inner saboteur that originates from our reptilian brain fight or flight response. It is designed to protect us, to warn us of dangers in life so that we can take action and survive.
- Trouble brews in life when we mix up messages from our saboteur, when we start paying too much attention to illogical fears and potential for emotional pain.
- We shoot ourselves in the foot, we become our own worst enemy by acting upon the command of our saboteur.
- Our saboteur lives in the unconscious mind and it influences our decisions. The more attention that we pay to it, the more that it thrives, and as a result we develop habitual limiting thinking and we live in a comfort zone.
- By recognising the involvement of your saboteur in your life you can start making new choices.
- Every time you push up against the edge of your comfort zone you expand it. This is how you will grow.
- Recognise when you are feeling unnecessary fear, recognise that it is your saboteur and this offers you new opportunities for a better life.

CHAPTER 8

Unwanted behaviour, addictions and our saboteur

At some stage in our lives we all develop some kind of unwanted behaviour. It is quite understandable when you think about it. The unconscious mind is unable to make decisions independently. It is our servant, it relies on our conscious instruction to give us what we have requested. **Our conscious instruction is where we focus our attention**. Based on where we are directing our attention, our unconscious mind will assist us in developing routines and habits to make achieving our goals easier.

The thing is that we do not always direct our attention towards what we want. We often direct our attention towards and away from what we do not want. This is where problems develop and at the heart of this is our saboteur.

Let us not forget that our saboteur is part of our flight or fight response from the reptilian brain. It has been developed with our good intention in mind: to protect us, to enable and to ensure our survival.

Addictions

Say for example we have developed a habit of eating too much **chocolate** and it is causing us to be overweight. Our overeating of chocolate has become an unwanted behaviour for us. In order to understand the behaviour it is useful for us go back to the beginning of the habit to have a look at how it can develop.

As anyone who likes chocolate will know, eating it in moderation can be a real pleasure. Chocolate contains a large quantity of sugar and so eating it can give you a temporary energy boost, making you feel better, increasing the level of serotonin and endorphins in your system. In periods of low energy or when you are feeling a bit low, then you reach for some chocolate and it makes you feel a bit better. This establishes the unconscious link between chocolate and receiving a reward. Next time you are feeling a bit low, and because the unconscious mind works with patterns, you may automatically go the the fridge for a quick fix chocolate boost. You again make the link between chocolate and a reward. Thus your chocolate habit has been born. You have trained your saboteur to seek reward via eating chocolate.

The thing is that the more frequently you focus your attention on chocolate, the more your unconscious mind makes that link to feeling better, the more chocolate you are going to eat to satisfy your saboteur. Eventually the whole process can become unconscious for you. You do not even need to consciously register feeling low in energy in order for you to go to the fridge, get some chocolate out and eat the lot. You can do it all without thinking.

Unfortunately, for the same reason that chocolate gives you a temporary boost in energy, it also means that if you eat a lot of it you gain weight. In addition to the sugar in chocolate, it also contains large quantities of fat which can clog up your system. If you are eating a lot of chocolate, then eventually you will probably make the conscious link between your being overweight and the amount of chocolate that you are eating. You will decide to eat less chocolate, or to cut it out altogether. Easier said than done.

Our unconscious mind will seek to serve us according to where we are focussing our attention. If we are thinking about chocolate frequently, then our unconscious mind is going to think that we want chocolate, thus increasing our desire to eat chocolate. It does not matter that we are thinking about not eating chocolate, our focus and attention is still on chocolate. Our unconscious mind does not understand negatives, our saboteur will require its reward. The only way to break out of this habit and this cycle of unwanted behaviour is to **direct our attention towards specifically what we want** and set up an alternative system of reward for our saboteur.

This is a typical example of how addictions work. You could substitute chocolate for cigarettes, or even hard drugs and the cycle is the same. We set up the unwanted behaviour out of a perceived need to feel better - a positive intention. We associate the behaviour with some kind of reward. It becomes an unconscious habit which is detrimental to us. We continuously seek more and more until it becomes an obvious problem for us and then we find it tricky to break the habit. We have set up a system of self sabotage.

Procrastination

Another form of unwanted behaviour may be **procrastination**. Perversely procrastination involves not doing anything but it is an unwanted behaviour all the same. When we are procrastinating then what are we doing in our head? In some way we are stuck, we are stuck and we can not find a way forward. We will tend to be thinking of all the things that we do not want to happen. We will be thinking of reasons not to take action.

Take someone who is procrastinating about doing household chores. What is the reason that they are not doing the household chores? It is probably because they are associating perceived pain with doing the chores. This may be because if they are doing the chores, then they are not able to be doing other things that may provide pleasure, like relaxing and watching TV. It may be because doing the chores seems particularly unpleasant, again this is moving away from pain. If we perceive that something is likely to be painful for us then it will trigger our saboteur and our fight or flight response.

As we neglect the household chores, so the house gets messier and messier and so the thoughts about doing the chores become more and more prominent in our minds. Everywhere we look, we see mess and this triggers our thoughts about doing the chores. In turn this triggers our saboteur as we associate pain with taking action. So, we sit down and watch TV, procrastinating about doing the chores. Every time we think about taking action we get a feeling of reluctance, this is our saboteur.

Eventually things will get so messy that we have a massive job to do in order to tidy the house. We will eventually take action because the pain associated with not doing the chores becomes greater than the pain associated with taking action. We are no longer procrastinating but we have been forced to take action. This will build our resentment towards the task and as we are doing it we will feel the pain, so strengthening our negative perception. This will make our reluctance even greater in future and make our procrastination worse.

This scenario applies equally to other areas of procrastination. If we are procrastinating over a piece of work that we need to do, the longer that we sit at our desk and procrastinate over it, the greater our reluctance towards doing it becomes. We build up resentment towards having to do it, building up the pain that we associate with it. Our flight of fight response takes place and we become angry, resentful or we get up and do something else, putting it off for another day.

The way to overcome procrastination is associate more pain with not taking action than we do with taking action, or better to associate pleasure with taking action thus rewarding our saboteur in a way that benefits us.

Being defensive

One of the causes of breakdowns in communication and poor relationships can be our propensity to be defensive. Whenever we feel criticised, challenged or we feel that someone else is better at something than we are then this can trigger our natural defense mechanism. Our natural defense mechanism is of course our friend the flight or fight response, our saboteur. Think about the word defense. Our flight or fight response is designed to defend us to ensure our survival. When we experience criticism, or a challenge to our supremacy, then the unconscious mind recognises the pattern in this as a threat to our survival. We seek to defend ourselves from the perceived attack.

Our being defensive can display itself as aggression towards other people, it can be exasperation, irritation and a lack of tolerance for other people and their perceived behaviour. We may find ourselves reacting angrily or we may seek to leave the situation and possibly the relationship if the behaviour continues.

The thing to bear in mind here is that we are talking about our perceptions again. Our perceptions will be formed based on past encounters, memories, beliefs about ourselves and others. When we *feel* criticised, then it may not necessarily be the case that we are being criticised, this is just our perception and we will act defensively. Our deletion, distortion and generalisation takes place in order to form our perception of being criticised. We end up with unwanted behaviour, communication failure and relationship struggles.

Is there anyone in your life that triggers a response from you that you do not want? It is worth remembering when thinking about this person that our perceptions are based on our own projections. If we are seeing something in another person that we do not like, then this is our projection. If someone is appearing to criticise us, then this may well be their saboteur, their defense mechanism showing itself in response to us. This is what we describe as being a "struggle". Our saboteurs are struggling for supremacy.

A client of mine, let's call her Jane, argues constantly with her mum. It is a two way thing. She describes it as "we get our backs up and we fight." Do not get me wrong, she loves her mum and her mum adores her but they fight like cat and dog. Whenever she picks up the phone to speak with her mum, Jane tells me that she has a resolve to be calm and to not let her mum provoke her. The conversation starts well, and then seemingly out of the blue the old feelings of irritation and exasperation emerge and the arguments start.

What is happening here? Well, when we dissect the conversation we realise that the trigger for the irritation normally arises with a similar pattern. Jane says that she feels that the questions in her conversation with her mum just go one way. She is doing all the asking. "How have you been?" "What have you been up to?" "What have you got planned?" She can have a whole conversation with her mum without her mum asking her any questions at all. This leads her to think that her mum does not care about her. The longer the conversation lasts, the more that this irritates her. The more that this feeling grows. Now this of course triggers her defense mechanism and her saboteur makes an appearance in the form of her feelings of irritation, frustration and annoyance. These feelings start to display in the conversation.

Her mum often discusses her problems with Jane. She does not have that many people to talk to and she obviously finds it good to have someone to talk with who listens to her. Jane will typically listen to the problems and then offer solutions. The problem is that her mum will bring up the same problems every time they speak together. This leads Jane to believe that her mum does not listen to her. This strengthens the emergence of her saboteur and furthers her irritation. Eventually she loses her temper and says something like, "I have already discussed this with you and I gave you a solution. You do not listen to me." Her mum, at this stage, feels under attack and her own defense mechanism sparks into life. She retaliates. "I do listen to you. It is you who doesn't listen." The argument starts.

Unconsciously, every time she picks up the phone to her mum or visits her, she is waiting for signals in the conversation that confirm what she has seen in the past. Signals that provide her with evidence that confirms her suspicion that her mum does not care about her and does not listen to her. Whenever she has her evidence, this stimulates her saboteur and provokes her negative reaction. The more times that this same situation occurs the more ingrained become the responses. Unless this pattern is interrupted, eventually, picking up the phone or meeting her mum will automatically provoke the reaction. She will associate pain with speaking with her mum and she may decide to speak with her less often.

Naturally these sorts of situations occur all the time and they will normally end up in the pattern being interrupted temporarily by the relationship becoming distant or a full blown confrontation where the feelings are shared and a way forward is agreed.

Thinking about situations at work, this type of breakdown in communication is frequent. There is a great deal of *self* invested in a work environment. Competition is fierce, the strongest thrive and survive and the most skilled get promoted and paid more.

One day you are sitting at work and your boss arrives. She walks straight past you, head down and walks into her office. She shuts the door. You think that she must have seen you. *Why did she not say hello? What have I done wrong? Oh, gosh I must be in trouble.*

At this stage you are unconsciously feeling under threat. Your saboteur is on high alert and all sorts of emotions are being stirred up. The main emotion is fear of course but you may just feel a bit uncomfortable. This sort of situation will naturally lead to you becoming defensive, the worst case scenario is that your livelihood is under threat. Survival is associated with livelihood, your fight or flight system is triggered.

Your boss calls you into her office. You fear the worst. How do you think that this conversation is going to go for you?

"About this piece of work," she holds up a document that you have put together for her.

This must have been why she was ignoring me.

"Yes, I know that it was not my best work, I apologise. Please give me a second chance. Give it me back and I will do it again. I'm so sorry." You defend yourself.

"What are you talking about? Actually I thought that it was excellent. Your best work to date. I have been thinking about how we can better utilise you and I wanted to discuss how we can recognise you better for your work. However, we should do something first of all about your confidence!"

Aaargh. I have shot myself in the foot. Thank you very much saboteur!

On another day someone who works for you calls you on the telephone. They start asking you about a decision that you made recently. "Can I just ask, why did you decide that?"

Your saboteur is of course listening in to this conversation. *Why are they asking me "why did I decide that?" Are they going to tell me that I made the wrong decision? Are they challenging my authority?*

Your defense mechanism takes over and you react defensively. "I decided that because it was the best thing for all concerned."

"Why did you decide that it was the best thing for all concerned?" They reply.

Are they being facetious? Are they trying to undermine me?

"Because it is my JOB to decide." Your saboteur tells them.

You react in a way that is born out of fear. In the eyes of your saboteur you have had a challenge to your authority, your fight mechanism is triggered and it will try to ensure your survival.

This response goes right back to instincts from our reptilian world. Fight for supremacy or die.

In reality this is a very extreme reaction and your reaction may well be much less aggressive in your defense. It is likely to be based on your perceived level of security on your job, whether you have had a succession of perceived challenges in the past and your feelings about your skill level. It may also depend on your perception of the skill level of the person asking you the question. Of course it may have been a completely innocent question born out of the persons desire to make sure that they understand what you want from them based on the decision that you made. They may be asking in order to give you what you want.

Positive Intention

One thing that is common to all of these unwanted behaviours is that they start with a positive intention. There is always a positive intention lurking somewhere behind any behaviour. Often the positive intention comes down to a need for survival in one form or another. What is in charge of our need to survive? Our reptilian brain and our saboteur.

We start a bad habit, like eating too much because it makes us feel better. Why do we want to feel better? What is the purpose for us behind feeling better? To have a better life, be happier, have a better level of survival.

We start procrastinating in order to avoid perceived pain. Why do we avoid pain? Because pain at the unconscious level is associated with a potential threat to our survival.

We are defensive, we get irritated with others, we get frustrated and annoyed because at some level we feel under threat. Our reptilian brain cannot distinguish between real threat and perceived threat and so we react in survival mode, fight or flight. Our intention is positive for us in that it is brought about by our need to protect ourselves, to survive.

Whenever we see other people behaving in a way that we do not like, whenever people act against us in some way, there is some kind of positive intention for them behind this behaviour. It may sometimes seem like a bit of a stretch to think about it this way as we need to see past our own saboteur in order to do it. Think about it, you may find that it is true.

I was listening to someone speak on the radio the other day. They had been mugged and hospitalised and they were telling their story. They had been minding their own business, putting some rubbish in their dustbin which was out on the street at the time, when someone rushed up to them and punched them on the jaw. It was a totally unprovoked attack and they stole the carrier bag which this person was carrying and which contained their rubbish. There seems to be some kind of trend of people doing this thing. It just seems senseless. However there is a positive intention in there somewhere. The mugger is presumably so devoid of other ways to gain food and money that they see the easiest way of feeding themselves as being to take from other people. This is about their perception of what is required for their survival. Furthermore, they do not want to risk someone putting up any resistance, they might get caught or even get hurt themselves, so they knock the person unconscious before they get a chance to fight. This is an extreme example of someones saboteur causing them and other people problems.

Even in *the* most extreme of situations people's behaviour is driven by a positive intention. In 2001 Armin Meiwes, a computer repair man from Germany advertised on the internet for someone to be eaten by him. Unbelievably he found someone who agreed to his request. They met up and Meiwes proceeded to chop off his victims penis. They ate the penis together before Meiwes killed his victim and ate a large amount of his flesh. Meiwes was caught and jailed. When he was asked why he did it, he said it was because he felt "lonely". His logic was that if he ate someone then he could never be separated from them and so would never be lonely again. This was his positive intention for himself.

The need for survival, existence, happiness and wealth are the prime drivers for unwanted behaviour with the reptilian brain flight or fight response being an underlying unconscious presence in that behaviour. We all have the potential to create unwanted behaviour, after all it starts at an unconscious level. Recognising what it is that we are doing that we do not want, recognising the source of the behaviour and understanding the reasons for it, put it in the light of our awareness and allow us to make better choices.

Key Points

- We create unwanted behaviours and addictions as a result of feeding our saboteur. We feed our saboteur by listening to it.
- When we focus on what we want then we tend to get it. The reverse is also true.
- Addictions result from a combination of a chemical process and habit. These things give our saboteur a perceived reward. The more we reward our saboteur, the more it demands. In this way we set up a system of self sabotage.
- We procrastinate as a result of a need to avoid some kind of perceived pain. We move away from doing things that we associate with pain and we move towards things that appear to reward us and give us pleasure.
- We overcome procrastination by associating more pleasure with taking action than we feel pain in doing the task.
- Many breakdowns in communication and relationships result from our being defensive.
- Being defensive is part of our flight or fight mechanism and is a product of our saboteur.
- Every behaviour has a positive intention and often that intention is born by a need to survive.
- Our saboteur sees it as its duty to help us to survive and sometimes it encourages us into activities that are unhelpful and dangerous.

- Our saboteur has a positive intention but it is not always steering us in the right direction.

CHAPTER 9

Anxiety, stress and depression

Negative emotions play a big part in reducing our overall level of happiness in life if they are allowed to build up. They can also be a source for anxiety, stress and depression. When I talk about a build up of negative emotions I am referring to negative emotions that occur in the first place as a result of something that happens in our life that we perceive to be negative for us.

Experiencing negative emotions is quite natural and they serve a positive purpose for us. Amongst other things they allow us to move away from things and events that are likely to cause us harm. A build up of negative emotions takes place when we fail to process the emotions that occurred from the original source. The unconscious mind recognises as one of its prime directives that negative emotions, when stored within us can become harmful to us. It forces us to confront stored negative emotions by representing them to us for resolution whenever it sees an opportunity. As long as we fail to address the negative emotions within us they will play a bigger and bigger part in our life thus affecting our happiness and the chemical balance in our bodies.

If we experience some kind of health scare in life as many of us do, then we may experience the negative emotion of fear. Of course, this is quite natural as we fear for our survival. This health scare can be considered a significant emotional event. The negative emotion of fear releases the steroid hormone of cortisol into our system. Cortisol acts to help us cope with short periods of stress by preventing the release of substances in the body that cause inflammation. It also enables us to direct our reserves of energy towards fighting disease and getting better rather than other less immediately necessary functions.

In short bursts then it is useful to experience fear in order for us to naturally produce the right chemicals to help us recover from illness and function at the same time. However, if the release of excess cortisol continues over a sustained period, if our fear continues to be present, then it can be harmful to us. Amongst other things, sustained excess cortisol in our system can lead to the weakening of the immune system, muscle wastage and a weakening of the bones.

We process our negative emotions by recognising and acknowledging them. When we acknowledge fear and we see a positive purpose for our fear, then we find that the fear reduces and goes away. When we fail to acknowledge fear, fail to accept it, when we ignore these negative emotions then they remain hidden within our system. They go underground but they are still there. The slightest thing can lead the negative emotion to resurface. This is often what we experience as anxiety and stress, an almost constant stream of negative emotion.

Anxiety

Think about what anxiety is. It is the constant creation of negative thoughts, fearful thoughts. We imagine that negative events are going to take place, this brings on our fear, this in turn stimulates our fight or flight response. As a result cortisol is pumped into our system. We are not creating these negative thoughts on purpose, they seem to come from nowhere, in fact they come from our unconscious mind. It is attempting to protect us. Always a positive intention, not always a positive result.

Like other forms of behaviour, thinking is habitual and negative thinking therefore is a habit. Habits can be changed by deliberately creating alternative behaviours. You are in charge of your thinking, first of all you must recognise what is taking place and then we can create other forms of default thinking that are more positive for you.

Worrying is a habit, nothing more. How much time in your past have you spent worrying about things that never happened? Worrying is a complete waste of time. Even if the imagined bad event does occur it will not have helped you at all by worrying about it. Imagining the worst case scenario is not a waste of time, it is otherwise called a risk assessment. Dwelling on the worst case scenario is pointless and destructive to you.

If you are worrying about something today then think about that thing now. What benefit will worrying give you? Will it protect you from the event occurring? When the time has past and the event was nothing like you are imagining now, then how will you feel about having spent time worrying about it today?

See worry as an opportunity to take positive action and you will be much better prepared for the events that lie ahead. What positive action can you take to ensure that you get the best possible outcome for you? Do it!

Worrying and anxiety are often a symptom of repressed negative emotions. If you suffer from either, then it will help you to process your deepest fears, the reason for your sadness, guilt, anger or hurt.

Stress

Stress is a completely natural physical reaction, a response to events in life. It is our body's way of responding to a challenge and the reaction is our fight or flight response. We see stress as a bad thing. What we perceive as stress is associated with negative feelings and therefore it is a negative thing for us. In actual fact stress over a short period of time can be a good thing for us.

Even the act of getting out of a chair creates stress in our body as our body is forced to react in order to allow us to stand up. Exercising, going to the gym, jogging, playing sport all create levels of stress and we build muscle as a result of the stress that we place on our body. Growth results not in the process of creating stress but the recovery from it. If we do not recover from periods of stress, then this is where the problems can occur.

There is a chemical process involved with stress. Cortisol is produced. Cortisol is known as the stress chemical. There are other neurotransmitters released as well, including seratonin and norepinephrine, which are both commonly associated with well-being. Once again there is positive intent involved in your body's response giving it the best possible chance of recovery from the threat.

Sustained exposure to stress in the body creates the feelings that we associate with stress and this is unpleasant and harmful to us in the long run. It creates a chemical imbalance in our system. This is known as chronic stress and the chemical imbalance that is created can result in the weakening of our immune system, high blood pressure, increased risk of strokes, depression and it can accelerate the aging process.

Physical stress recovery takes place when we rest. So we must rest our body from time to time, put our feet up. Of course stress is not only caused by physical exertion, it is caused also by mental exertion. Mental exertion can take place as a result of continuous worrying, dwelling on past mistakes, past negative events. Continually experiencing negative emotions will cause stress, as will anxiety about the future.

In order to recover from periods of mental stress we must communicate to our body that we have resolved our negative emotions. We must calm our mind, ceasing the worry and anxiety cycles that take over our thoughts. **We must rest our minds**, this will recreate the right chemical balance and we will start feeling better. Resting our minds does not necessarily mean taking time off work, it can do but it does not necessitate this. It is something that we can do without the need to remove ourselves from every day life, it just means giving ourselves a break from our habitual negative thinking. We are going to explain how you can do this in later chapters of this book.

Depression

One of the possible end results of excessive worrying, anxiety and stress is depression. Depression is normally experienced as persistent low moods, and accompanied by lack of self-esteem and a lack of appreciation for normally enjoyable activities. Clinical depression has several possible treatments which may involve prescription of anti-depressant drugs, the provision of counselling, cognitive behavioural therapy and exercise.

American psychiatrist, Aaron Beck is the originator of Cognitive Behavioural Therapy (CBT). He proposed that three problems underlie depression: negative thoughts about oneself, ones environment and ones future, recurrent patterns of depressive thinking, and distorted information processing. Essentially these are the things that we have been talking about in this book. How we delete, distort and generalise our experiences to form our model of the world. How we create habits, recurrent thinking. How we generate negative results for ourselves by failing to process negative emotions. CBT aims to assist people in these three areas, by addressing these same areas this book aims to do the same.

Many cases of depression result from significant emotional events, such as the death of a close relative. Of course it is not the event itself that creates the depression, more the failure to release the build up of negative emotions associated with the event. This is what we have been referring to as the processing of our negative emotions.

Once any negative emotions that have been built up are released, people tend to feel free again to feel positive emotions. They are able to look on the "brighter side of life", appreciate the "here and now" rather than being stuck in the past. Positive emotions involve the release of the mood enhancing neurotransmitters of serotonin, dopamine and norepinephrine. These are the same chemicals that are in the anti-depressant drugs and the same chemicals that are released as a result of exercise.

We will use the example of the death of a loved one to enable you to understand the process that takes place with someone getting depression. When we lose someone close to us then it is quite normal to experience a huge sense of loss. We know that life is never going to be the same again and we know that we can not do anything about that. With this loss comes a great deal of hurt and sadness. Sadness at not being able to see, hear or touch the person again. Hurt because we feel damaged by the loss, we feel like our heart is broken. There is also a possibility that there is some guilt involved. We may feel guilty that it was them and not us that died. We may feel guilty that we did not do for them or say the things to them that we now want to do or say. There may also be anger that they were taken from us. Anger at the unfairness of it all.

After the loss we go through a mourning period where we experience all of these negative emotions, we are consumed by thoughts of our loved one. We remember things involving them from the past and we struggle to think about our future without them. Every single one of our thoughts brings with it negative emotions. We are anxious and we are stressed. When we wake up in the morning we start with thoughts of our loss, they continue all day and we go to bed at night with these thoughts. If we are lucky then we go to sleep, otherwise we lie awake thinking about how we wish things were different.

Eventually we may start noticing that the negative thoughts are reducing in frequency and the emotions are less strong. We begin to notice some positives in life. We are able to appreciate a beautiful sunny day. We notice the beauty in nature and we notice the smiles on the faces of small children. We remember what joy feels like. This will happen when we reach a stage of acceptance. When we start accepting that things will never be the same again, accepting that the loved one has gone, then we start recovering from this stress. We do not forget, we will never forget but we accept the loss. This allows us to move forward.

In some people acceptance does not occur as a natural progression of events. The negative thinking continues, becomes habitual. The stress and anxiety continue and can actually appear to get worse. We start losing energy as the stress continues, the thoughts take our energy away from us. We start feeling like we cannot move forward in life, in fact we do not have a future at all. When we look forward we just see darkness, and gloom. We lose confidence as we feel worthless, useless. We continue to spend time thinking about the person that we have lost and the negative emotions persist. This is when we are in depression. Some people describe depression as a world full of blackness. No future. No beauty. Just horrible dark thoughts, being in our head is the worst place on earth.

And there is hope. Because people do recover from depression. It can just start with one less negative thought. It starts with one glimpse of light. It starts with a slightly better day. It comes with understanding what is making us depressed and it starts with the knowledge of what actions we can take in order to get the recovery process underway.

One of my clients described depression as "Cantbebotheredyitis". Nothing seems important. Self care often suffers as people cannot be bothered to look after themselves. This client described her recovery from depression as starting one day with the decision to have a bath and shave her legs. This simple act of self care changed her perspective on herself and her life. It improved her self image and bit by bit she began piecing her life back together.

Maybe recovery is sparked by something as simple as someone suggesting that we take some exercise. A walk to the shops. Exercise does help people recover from depression, anxiety and stress. Maybe we learn how to be mindful, there are some instructions on how to do that in the mindfulness exercises in this book. Mindfulness helps us connect with the here and now and is known to produce the same sort of feel good chemicals as exercise and anti-depression medication. Whatever it is that sparks the recovery, make no mistake it has to come from within. If we wait to recover before taking action then it will not happen.

By becoming aware of how we create our perceptions, we are able to challenge them. By becoming aware of the contribution of our saboteur in our life, the positive intention behind our fight or flight response we are able to recognise when it assists us and when it may be hindering us. By recognising the part played by our negative emotions in protecting us and healing, we are able to ensure that we no longer ignore them and store them up. By making plans and setting ourselves achievable goals, we get to design our future the way that we want it. By shining our light of awareness on these things we are able to see a clearer, brighter path to our future happiness.

Key points

- Negative emotions are created by events in our lives that are unpleasant for us. We store negative emotions in our bodies when we fail to address them at source. Our unconscious mind keeps bringing up stored negative emotions to enable us to deal with them but we often ignore the signals. We release stored up negative emotions by recognising and acknowledging them. Stored up negative emotions of fear and anger can cause anxiety, stress and depression.
- Negative thinking is a habit and worrying is nothing more than negative thinking. We can break habits by deliberately

creating alternative behaviours. We overcome worry and anxiety by facing up to our thoughts and challenging them.
- We see stress as a bad thing. Stress is a natural phenomenon, we build muscle by placing stress on our bodies and letting them recover. Stress is negative for us and causes health problems when we fail to recover from the thing that is causing us stress. When we build in processes of recovery then we can grow from stress. Processes of recovery from physical stress can involve rest and relaxation of our body. Processes of recovery from mental stress can involve mindfulness exercises as we discuss later in this book.
- Three problems generally underlie depression: negative thoughts about ourselves, our environment and our future, recurrent patterns of depressive thinking, and distorted information processing. We are addressing each of these aspects in this book.
- Depression normally starts when we fail to accept certain life events, such as the death of a loved one. Failure to accept (and release the negative emotions) leads to us getting stuck in the past. We suffer from recurring negative thought patterns and this spirals down into depression as it affects our energy and health.
- Mindfulness helps us with acceptance of the moment and helps us to recover from depression, anxiety and cycles of worry.

Part 2 - Beginning to shape your future

CHAPTER 10

Values and Beliefs

One of the main determining factors of your future success, sense of well-being and happiness is the belief and values structure that you have in your life.

Your beliefs and values are largely unconscious within you and they form the rules that you lay down for your life. These are the rules that your unconscious mind uses in order to filter information and provide you with your perceptions and your internal representations. They also act as a driver for your behaviour, they provide your motivation to do something or your motivation to avoid doing something.

Beliefs are what you believe to be true in the world and what you believe to be true for and about you. For example, "I believe that I can help people to be more successful," is a belief that I have. It is true for me.

Values are things that are important to you, what you value in your life. **Helping people** is important to me, so "helping people" is one of my values.

They act as rules and determine behaviour because you will tend to move towards things that are important to you. Helping people is important to me, so in my life I look for ways to help people, through my work and in my social life. I have a belief that supports me in doing this, as I believe that when I help people I can assist them in being happier and more successful. This belief encourages me to take action in this area. If I believed that I did not have the skills to help people, nothing to add, then this belief would deter me from taking action. I would probably do something else instead.

There is no doubt that genetics plays a part in happiness, personality and intelligence although there is much debate over to what extent it makes a difference. Beliefs and values do not come from genetics, they will shape your personality and levels of happiness and they may well come from your mum and dad.

Morris Massey, in his book, *The People Puzzle - Understanding yourself and others* proposes that most of our values are formed in the first seven years of our life. He calls this our Imprint Period. During this period we are like a sponge absorbing information. We adopt an imprint of the way that the world looks and works. The people that are around us share their views of the world with us, their values and beliefs and we adopt them as our own.

If you think of who was around you when you were young, then we may be talking about your mum and dad, your friends, your school teachers, your siblings. All of these people will have shared with you their values and beliefs. They will have acquired their own values and beliefs in the same way. This is one of the reasons why cultures form and why you become like the people that you spend most of your time with.

By the age of seven our imprint has formed and we begin modelling others, copying behaviour, using our acquired values and beliefs as rules for what we do. We continue to acquire values and beliefs and our experiences, our successes and failures, enable us to form some of our own.

Over our lifetime we may acquire beliefs and values from religion, from groups that we belong to, from the media, and from society. These are all significant possible influences on us.

I acquired several values from my mum and dad when I was a child that I still have today and that have played a prominent part in my life. My mum was always preaching **honesty, loyalty, hard work** and **contribution** to others. These are things that are important to her, things that were important to her parents and positive things that have been important to me too. I adopted another of her values, **security**. Whilst it is still in the back of my mind I made a deliberate decision several years ago to make this value less important to me, as I felt that it was holding me back from being a success. Security for me led to me staying in my comfort zone, I decided that **progress** was more important to me than security and this is how I now prioritise. My motivation is now towards progress and in the back of my mind I make a study of the possible consequences of progress, which satisfies my lesser value of security. I find that this generally keeps me on the straight and narrow!

Events in life also help shape our values system. Our values and beliefs can change over time as we develop our learning and new skills. We create new beliefs about our ourselves and our capabilities by learning and developing new skills. My belief that I can help people to become more successful has developed over a period of time as I have experienced coaching people and observed their successes. My ability to coach people was developed over a significant number of years in my life where I acquired the necessary qualifications, learning and practice. I have not always had this belief but it has been developed and I now have evidence for it, which leads me to believe that it is true.

Significant events may lead us to change what we believe is important to us. For example, if we have had a partner that has been unfaithful to us and this has ruined the relationship, then loyalty and honesty may become very important to us in terms of future relationships. They may not have been criteria that had stood out as particularly important to us in the past. We may not have vetted past partners based on those criteria, but we will be looking out for those criteria to be met in future before we enter a relationship.

We do not walk around with these values and beliefs etched on our foreheads, they are not apparent to other people other than through our actions and words. At the same time they are not necessarily always apparent to us to either. Until I discovered my values using the process that I am going to explain to you I did not go about my life thinking, **honesty, loyalty and hard work** all the time. When I was deciding to do something I did not consciously think, *does that fit in with my values and beliefs?* My process of deciding included my values and beliefs but that part was unconscious. I filtered the information on the table in front of me via my memories, previous decisions, values and beliefs. The decision that I made was probably in line with my highest values and my beliefs but was made based on other logic, pros and cons. This is probably the same for you now.

Sometimes, when we make decisions that do not sit particularly comfortably with us, then this may be because we are acting in conflict with our values. In situations where we are forced into doing something, where the decision is out of our hands, then this may sit awkwardly with us for the same reason.

Values tend to be less conscious than beliefs. We are more likely to know what our beliefs are, and we will verbalise them from time to time. Values tend to remain hidden and only display themselves in our behaviour.

We have therefore a whole system of criteria that sits inside of us, rules that our unconscious mind uses to determine our actions and our future, and it may all be based on other people's views of what is important and true. Isn't that scary? We may live our whole lives and never consciously discover what our primary values are even though we make all our decisions based upon them.

The good news is that I am going to share a process with you that we can use to bring them into our conscious awareness so that we get to know what they are. Bearing in mind what we want to achieve in our life, how we want our life to be, we can identify our values and ensure that they support us. If we have values that we do not want, then we can eliminate them. If we decide that a certain value should be present and is not currently there, then we can add it in. This is one way to ensure that our mind filters are set up to give us the results that we want, so that we get our life the way that we want it. Does that sound like something that you might like to do?

If you are still wondering what values are specifically, then think of them as concepts. They tend to be represented by ambiguous words or an ambiguous collection of words. They are words that mean different things to different people.

Take **fun,** for example. Fun can mean a different thing to me from what it means to you. In order to have fun I may have to do different things from those that you need to do in order to have fun. Fun is a value because it can be important to someone. **Respect** is another value. In order to show me that you respect me, you may need to do different things to the things that other people need to do in order for you to respect them. Respect may be different in nature to me from what it is to you. This is due to our generalisation, distortion and deletion again. It does not matter what your interpretation is, as long as you understand what it means to you.

Key Points

- We live by an unconscious set of rules that are formed by our values and our beliefs.
- We inherit many of our values and beliefs from the people that we spent our time with when we were young: parents and friends.
- We tend to develop sets of beliefs around things that we see as being important to us, our values.

- Whilst we can change our values, mostly we fail to do this and they remain unconscious to us, silently guiding us to our destiny.

CHAPTER 11

Discovering your values

Stage 1 in Shaping your Future

Here is the process:

1) Go grab a pen and a blank piece of paper.
2) The question that I would like you to think about is: what is important to you currently in your life? Just trust your unconscious mind to tell you what these things are. Ask yourself "What is important to me in my life?" I suggest that you write down the things that spring to mind. Create a list.
3) Once you have a few things on your list, ask yourself, "What else is important to me?" Write these things down.
4) Then ask yourself "What motivates me?" Write the things that spring to mind down. We want things that motivate you now, things that are important to you now, not things that you would like to be important or things that you would like to have motivate you.

   Do you have your list? Great.

5) Now what I would like you to do is look at your list and put

the values in order of importance to you. Start with the most important, then the next, then the next. Rewrite your list in the order of importance.

Once you have your list in hierarchical order we are going to evaluate your values to ensure that they support you.

There is no right or wrong order. Everyone is unique and we all want different things in life, so you can expect your list to be different from mine. The most important thing is that you recognise that this list will likely be driving your behaviour, good and bad. So it is important that going forward it supports you in getting you to where you want to go.

How does your list of values look to you? When you review your list now is there anything missing? Is there anything that you would like to make important to you that is absent? If there is, then add it to your list.

Here is a snapshot of my list of values that I have currently:
Progress
Love
Health
Success
Contribution
Fun
Honesty
Fitness

There are other things that I could have on there but they are less important to me. These are my top values. Remember that my values will mean different things to you from what they mean to me.

Validating your list

In order to validate the order of my list. I start at the top and ask myself the question, "If I have **Love** and no **Progress** is that ok for me?" My answer is "no". That is not ok.

I check, "If I have **Progress** and no **Love** is that ok?" Yes, just about. Therefore I know that **Progress** is my top value.

I go down the list asking the same questions. "If I have **Health** and no **Love** is that ok for me?" My answer is "no". That is not ok.

I check, "If I have **Love** and not great **Health** is that ok?" Yes, just about. Therefore I know that **Love** is more important to me than **Health**.

Take your top two values and ask yourself the same questions. "If I have Value 2 and not Value 1 is that ok?" If your answer is "No" then you that you have the correct top value.

Just check it. Ask yourself, "If I have Value 1 and not Value 2 is that ok?"

If you have answered "No." Then it may be that you need to switch the values around on the list.

You now have a list of values that will guide you in your decision making. Keep the list with you, refer to it on a regular basis, this will ensure that you are aligning your life to your biggest principles. Review your list from time to time to make sure that it remains accurate for you and empowering for you. Become aware of the consequences of your values for you and other people around you. Change your list if it is not working for you in the way that you want it to.

Designing action points

Bear in mind now that your current level of satisfaction in life, even your happiness, will be influenced by the actions that you are taking in respect of your values.

In terms of my values list, I know that if I am making **progress**, if I am showing and receiving **love,** if I have good **health** in my life, this will have a big impact on how happy I am.

The best way that I can ensure that I am happy in my future is to take action now in each of these areas. I cannot necessarily do anything about my current levels of progress, love, and health but if I plan and take action in each of these areas, then I know that I will improve my life. This will instantly make me happier now and provide me with evidence of how I can achieve continued and improving happiness in future.

For example, if we take my value of **progress**. I can look at my life and say to myself "what have I got planned that is going to help me **progress**?"

When I think about this, then I think about **progress** in several areas of my life. My work, my personal development, my business. There are others, like **progress** in my relationships, my fitness, but they are covered by my other values.

I review each of the areas of my life where I would like **progress** and I look to see what actions, events, meetings I have got lined up that will help me **progress**. As I review these areas other things spring to mind that I can do, so I write these down. "What specifically do I need to do? How? By when? With whom?" I plan and I write down my actions.

Your actions may be huge, in terms of really transforming your lifestyle, or they may just be little tweaks to get you moving in the right direction.

There may be one or two values in your list where you are struggling to find suitable actions. When I talk about actions, it may be that the action is physical, for example, taking some exercise in the area of **health** or **fitness** if they are on your list. Actions may mean planning a schedule, or taking some time out to write in a journal to get to know yourself better. Getting to know your saboteur in a 'values' area such as **personal development**.

Actions do not always have to involve a specific physical action. Let's say that one of your values is **gratitude**. It may be that in relation to a value like this your actions are mental exercises such as, every morning before breakfast spending two minutes contemplating what you are grateful for in your life.

Your actions may be responsive. You may decide that you are going to spend the week ahead with a certain attitude in mind. For example, your action may be to recognise when you are feeling defensive as you communicate with others, thus enabling you to react in a different way. Or you may decide that you are going to spend the week with a purely positive mindset, observing negative thoughts when they arise and replacing them with positive ones.

Assessing beliefs

It is also useful to look at your values and notice what beliefs you have about yourself that are associated with that value or the actions that you would like to take around that value. Beliefs about yourself are normally identified by sentences starting with "I can..." "I can't.." "I am able to.." "I am unable to.." "I am .." "I am.. not"

I can write down a list of beliefs that I have about my **progress**. Some of them may be positive beliefs and others may be limiting beliefs. For example I might say "I can't progress at work because ..." I then need to assess this limiting belief and work out what I can do to change it.

If I said "I can't progress at work because the economy is no good." Then I need to look at the reason that I have this belief, my evidence. It does not support me and it does not necessarily have to be true. Other people are progressing in the same economy, so what do I need to think in order to change this belief?

If I said "I can't progress at work because I do not have the skills." Then, what do I need to learn? What training do I need to take in order to gain the skills? I then create an action to look into some suitable training. I book a training course, or I book time out to read and learn.

Limiting beliefs come from your saboteur and they really get in the way of you moving towards your values. They limit you and they do not have to be true. If they are not true for other people, then they do not have to be true for you. Question your limiting beliefs, thus questioning your saboteur. Ask yourself "When did I decide that?" "What do I need to change or how do I need to change for this to be different?" This will produce some more action points for you.

Summary of the process of Stage 1 in Shaping your Future

1) Ask yourself: "What is important to me in my life?" Create a list.
2) Once you have a few things on your list, ask yourself: "What else is important to me?" Write these things down.
3) Then ask yourself: "What motivates me?" Write the things that spring to mind down.
4) Once you have your list put the values in order of importance to you. Start with the most important, then the next, then the next. Rewrite your list in the new order of importance.
5) Validate your list - Ask yourself: "If I have Value 1 and not Value 2 is that ok?" "If I have Value 2 and not Value 1 is that ok?" Work your way down your list in this way.
6) Design action points for each value on your hierarchy. Ask yourself: "What have I got planned that is going to help me (Value 1)?" Work your way down your list creating actions.
7) Check your beliefs around each of your values. Ask yourself: "What do I believe about myself in terms of (Value 1)?" Work your way down your list of values.
8) Identify any limiting beliefs. Question them. "When did I decide that?" "What do I need to change or how do I need to

change for this to be different?" Create relevant actions.

Congratulations! You should now have a hierarchy of values and some associated actions. This is an exercise in designing a lifestyle, one that is going to make you happier and one that will ensure that you are living to your biggest principles. This will give you an uplifting feeling, one of integrity.

Examine your motivation - Are you moving towards what you want or away from what you do not want?

It is well worth noticing the input of your saboteur in this process. Your saboteur will want to resist some of the actions that you are planning, it will want to obstruct any level of change that you are bringing into your life.

Your saboteur is keen to keep you in your comfort zone, where it is safe. Thoughts of anything new and unknown are likely to provoke it into action. You may start feeling a little uncomfortable as a result, feeling yourself resisting taking action, resisting the changes. Recognise this as the involvement of your saboteur.

The next step in the process will help us identify where your saboteur is already playing a part in shaping your future.

What I am going to ask you to do is examine your values to see what motivation there is behind each one. In order to do this we are going to ask the question: "Why is that value important to me?"

Motivation can be positive or negative. Motivation towards doing something or motivation away from doing something.

Motivation to lose weight

For example, if someone is overweight, then they may be motivated to lose weight in order to feel better in themselves, feel better about themselves, look more attractive to other people. These are positive motivations. They are motivated towards achieving results that are positive for them. There is no apparent saboteur involvement here.

Someone who is overweight may also be motivated to lose weight in order to avoid health problems, or because they think that they look unattractive and they do not feel great in themselves. These are negative motivations. They are motivated away from things that they do not want. The saboteur is involved here. The motivation in this case is based upon fear. Fear of health problems, fear of appearing unattractive to others.

There is a big difference between wanting to look more attractive and wanting to look less unattractive? We will explain the reason for this shortly.

The problem with motivation away from something negative is that the motivation may not last. If someone is motivated to lose weight due to concerns over their health and this is their focus, then it may be a great incentive to start losing weight, it may shift them off a position of inactivity. However, when they start losing weight, then their motivation may well disappear as the apparent likelihood of a serious health problem reduces.

In this case there may be a period of time where weight loss occurs as the motivation is high and they are taking actions to reduce their weight. However, their motivation to take action will reduce as they lose weight and as it becomes less important to them. They become less scared of having a health problem and so they will be less compelled to take the continued actions necessary to lose weight. This may well result in them beginning to gain weight again. We see this all the time with people going on a diet and then quickly regaining the weight that they lost. They will, of course, at some stage become scared for their future health again and this will motivate them to start retaking actions, their flight response to fear. It becomes a cycle of losing and regaining weight.

Not ideal.

If someone is motivated to lose weight to achieve a positive result, for example to feel better in themselves, then the results will be different. They will start to take action, they will lose a bit of weight and they will recognise that they feel a bit better in themselves. They will realise that the more actions they take, the better they feel, the more weight that they lose. Remember that exercise is really powerful in assisting with the feel good factor, as it stimulates the release of the chemicals: dopamine, serotonin and noradrenaline. So, taking exercise will make them feel better, thus enabling them to feel that they are rewarded in two respects; they feel better and they are achieving their desired result of losing weight. This will encourage them to stay motivated, carry on taking action and carry on losing weight.

Stress reduction

The same principles apply with all values and all goals. The key is to design a focus that will get you the long term results that you want. Take stress reduction. If we are feeling stressed and we set ourselves a target of **reducing the feeling of stress in our life**, then we set off in pursuit of a negative.

We are currently stressed and we want less stress. We can adopt some relaxation routines, which will start to enable us to feel better.

As we begin to relax mentally and physically, so the stressed muscles in our brain and body get the period of recuperation that they require. We start to feel better as the chemical balance in our body improves. We stop pumping cortisol into our system. As we relax, so the body releases dopamine and serotonin, making us feel better. As we start to feel better, so the motivation to continue the relaxation techniques reduces. We do them with less and less frequency, eventually we stop the techniques altogether. We continue to feel better for a while as we benefit from the improved chemical balance. Unconsciously we think, *our job is done.*

Fundamentally we haven't changed. The behaviours that produced the stress in the first place are still ingrained in us, we have achieved a temporary improvement. It is only a question of time before we relapse into stress.

On the other hand. If we are feeling stressed and we determine to set about changing our lifestyle with the aim of achieving **a daily feeling of serenity**, then this is a positive objective. We design a lifestyle that incorporates the relaxation techniques, we know that this is a lifestyle choice for our future. We may also make other changes, such as examining the way that we respond to others. We may decide to write a regular journal in order to explore our feelings and emotions, to get to know our saboteur. Our focus is on a daily feeling of serenity. We start to feel better as our actions begin paying off. We experience our first glimpse of that feeling of serenity. We realise that there is so much more to come. Our motivation remains high as we feel the rewards from our relaxation techniques. The more we do, the more motivated we become to move towards our goal.

After a period of days the new habits start becoming unconscious. The new behaviours become part of us and it becomes easier and easier to achieve a feeling of well-being. Our whole attitude improves. Memories of our stress fade as the glimpses of the feelings of serenity get longer and longer. We continue to move towards our objective of a daily feeling of serenity. We send messages to our unconscious mind: *I love this new feeling. I want more of this. This is the way that I want to lead my life from now onwards.* This is how we create lasting improvement through change and through setting positive objectives.

Key Points

- Use our process to discover your values.
- Once the values have been revealed we can then set about

putting them in a hierarchy. Evaluate the hierarchy to ensure that it works for you.
- This process allows you to align your life to your biggest principles.
- You can refer to this list of values to assist you with future decision making. In this way you will start to design your life and get it the way that you want it.
- Once you have your hierarchy of values you can start designing actions that will enable you to get more of the things that are important to you in life and move towards taking control of your life.
- Assess beliefs around different areas of your life. This has the value of revealing limiting beliefs. Limiting beliefs hold us back, we hold them as facts and they limit our development and growth.
- Design actions to overcome your limiting beliefs.

CHAPTER 12

Identifying the direction of your motivation

Stage 2 in Shaping your Future

In order to identify whether you are moving towards what you want or away from what you do not want we can ask a simple question:

"Why is (a value) important to me?"

Take my top value of **progress**. If I ask myself the question of "Why is **progress** important to me?" Then I think "**Progress** is important to me because it will enable me to help more people, to make a bigger contribution. It will assist me in reaching my true potential."

This is really empowering for me. It gives me a sense of excitement. It is a really positive motivation for me. This is enabling me to shape my life the way that I want it.

If however, I thought "**Progress** is important to me because it will mean that I do not get complacent," then this is a negative motivation. I would be moving away from being complacent.

In developing this motivation around the value of **progress** it may be that I had slipped into a period of complacency. Quite unconsciously I may recognise that I am being complacent and this may set off my saboteur. I may start unconsciously fearing the consequences of being complacent. I will know deep down that this is not what I want. In this case I am motivated away from complacency by **progress**. As soon as I start making progress, then I will not feel complacent anymore. This will satisfy my saboteur and I will become less motivated to make further **progress**. In this way my progress will become intermittent.

It is a really subtle difference but one that could result in very different outcomes in my life.

Stage 2 in the process of shaping your future therefore is to ask yourself the question: "Why is (value) important to me?"

Start at the top of your list of values. Take the value and ask yourself the question: "Why is (value) important to me?"

Work your way down your list making a note of the answer that springs to mind for each value.

When you have your list then we need to assess which of your values you are moving towards in your motivation, and which of your values you are moving away from.

If any of your answers involve a negative, then you know that you are moving away. If you have phrases like "so that I do not", "so that I will not" or "so that I get less of" then this identifies the direction of your motivation as being away from what you do not want.

With each respective value make a note of "Away" or "Towards" next to the reason why it is important to you.

You will then have a list that starts by looking like this:

1) Progress - Progress is important to me because it will enable me to help more people, to make a bigger contribution. It will assist me in reaching my true potential - (Towards)

2) Value - Reason - (Towards/Away)

..and so on.

Getting in charge of your state

What may not be apparent to you yet is how you represent your values to yourself in your head. Bear in mind that we store memories as sounds, feelings, pictures, tastes and smells in our head. Together they provide us with our internal representations. Our memories are a collection of internal representations that we can recall and recreate specific moments in time in our mind.

When we recall a vivid memory with emotion in it, then we recall the emotion as well. Let's say that we recall a time in the past when we were around other people and we were having fun. When we remember that time we can recall what we saw at the time, what people said and how we felt - this is our internal representation. If we carry on remembering fun times then this can lift our mood, our state.

In the same way, if we are constantly thinking about negative things that have happened to us in the past, then we get internal representations associated with those times and it can start making us feel low. It can start bringing up negative emotions and we can get into a negative state.

You can get in positive charge of your state at any point in time simply by recalling memories of good times. So if you wanted to create a happy state, then flood your mind with thoughts of times in the past when you were really happy. If you wanted to feel motivated, then recall specific times in the past when you were feeling motivated, remember what you were seeing, hearing and feeling at the time. Hold this thought in your mind. This will make you feel motivated now.

Let us test this out:

- Can you recall a time in the past when you were really relaxed?
- Remember this time now. A specific time in the past when you were really relaxed.

You may need to read these instructions and then shut your eyes to really get back to that time.

- Just let your mind wander back to that time now and see what you saw, hear what you heard and really feel the feelings of being totally relaxed.
- Hold that thought in mind.

How do you feel? More relaxed? Great. Whenever you want to feel more relaxed you can go back to that time in your mind's eye, see what you saw, hear what you heard, feel what you felt and feel more relaxed instantly. If you need to close your eyes, then do that. Just make sure that you are not driving when you do it!

You can use this technique for lots of other positive states as well. For example, if you want to feel more confident, then remember a time in the past when you felt really confident. Remember a specific time in the past when you felt really confident. Float back to that time now in your mind and see what you saw, hear what you heard and really feel the feelings of being totally confident. Now, how does THAT feel? Excellent!

I use this state control technique whenever I am about to go and do a presentation. How do you think that it would be going into a presentation feeling really relaxed and confident? Now you know.

Bear in mind that the opposite is also true: you can get in a negative state just by doing the same process and recalling a negative event in the past. I do not recommend that you do it, but this is one of the reasons. This is one of the reasons that people get depressed, they keep thinking of negative events in the past and they keep associating with the negative feelings that thinking about those events brings.

As well as in past memories, we can also create internal representations of things that we expect to happen or would like to happen in the future.

I enjoy going hill walking and I can imagine now going on a walk in the future. I can see myself reaching the top of the hill that I am thinking about. As I think about this time in the future I can feel the feelings of warmth that I get from the waterproof jacket that I am wearing. I can feel the wind blowing on my cheeks. I can hear the wind as well. I can feel the feelings of satisfaction as I get to the summit. All of this creates a future memory. It might not be your cup of tea but when I think about it I want to get up and go right now!

As well as thinking about positive future events we can do the same thing with negative thoughts of the future. If I really want to I can think about some negative possibilities in going for a walk. I can imagine going for a walk up the same hill. I can imagine it raining as I climb up the hill. I can imagine the rain seeping into my jacket. The waterproofing on the jacket has failed. I can hear the squelch of my sodden feet as I tread my way through the mud. I can imagine shivering as I walk. It is misty and I cannot see my way ahead. I lose track of the path and I get lost. I am miserable.

Thinking these negative thoughts leaves me feeling less positive about hill walking. I might leave it until the weather improves!

When I think about hill walking I have a choice over how I think about it. I have a choice over how I imagine things going in the future for me. As it is one of my pastimes it is simple to think positively about it. When I think about doing something that I tend to enjoy less, like household chores for example, then it is trickier for me to have positive future thoughts about it.

This is the reason why it is so important to plan events for your future that you perceive as being positive for you. Leisure time, time with friends, time with family.

Worry

Anxiety and worry are simply recurring memories of future events where we are creating negative internal representations. If we are in a negative frame of mind then we are in danger of constantly seeing problems occurring in the future, things going wrong. This is supposed to be our internal protection mechanism at work but it is in fact self sabotage. It will make us worry all the more, it will bring us negative emotions and we will feel worse. This is how the worry habit can get a hold of us. Once we are in the grip of the worry habit then it takes a conscious effort to turn our thinking around.

I go jogging quite frequently. I am lucky to live on the edge of the countryside, so I can run from my house onto the surrounding moors. The moors are great for mountain biking, walking, running and lots of people use the moors to take their dogs for a walk. If you have ever gone running somewhere where there are dogs off the lead, then you will know that for some reason the dogs get really excited at the sight of someone running. They will often bound up to me when they see me and jump up. Mostly they are completely harmless, but some look ferocious and I get concerned about getting bitten on my bare legs!

Before I go for a run I sometimes think about the possibility of dogs biting me. It does not put me off but it could do if I let it and if it is playing on my mind. If I start thinking about it before I go for a run, then it can play on my mind all of the way through my run. I can start worrying about being bitten.

Let's think about the mental process I go through here. Unconsciously I am imagining the possibility of being bitten. This means that I am creating pictures in my head of dogs running up to me and biting me. Of course this stimulates my fight or flight response and I sense an underlying feeling of discomfort, brought about by fear. As I go for my run I am on high alert for any dogs that I may see. My train of thought leads to repeated thoughts of dogs coming up to me and biting me.

Once I have started thinking this way, then somehow I need to break out of this mode of thinking otherwise I can spend the whole of my jogging time worrying about something that is not likely to happen. As long as the thoughts persist I am not fully enjoying my run. I am on edge, anxious. I then see what I think is a dog in the distance. Fear strikes me. I get goosebumps, I slow down. As I get closer I realise that what I thought was a dog is in fact a bush. Silly me. I carry on with my run, anxiously.

All of this experience has been created in my mind based on past memories, decisions. I am deleting, distorting and generalising through my mind filters to create my current unpleasant reality.

Most of the time I do not think about dogs before I go running. I can go through the whole run without a single thought of dogs. Instead I am enjoying the fresh air, the countryside, listening to the birds in the trees. On these occasions the same external events have occurred but my experience has been completely different.

Triggers

It is easy to believe that we do not have control over our thinking, that we get what we are given. This is not the case. We set up neurological links to experiences that trigger automatic patterns of thinking. The key is to recognise what these triggers are so that we can we can determine how we react to them.

I now recognise that before I go for a run I can think about what I do not want, that is dogs running up to me, or I can think about getting fresh air and being in the countryside. It is my choice and my enjoyment depends on it. If I think about dogs, then I will be in an anxious state. If I think about being in the countryside and getting fresh air, then I will be in a relaxed state. It is my choice.

Triggers to repetitive thinking can be set up by a single experience or it can take several similar experiences to set up the link. It all depends on the strength of the experience. One thing is certain, the more frequently that we trigger the thoughts, the more automatic they become.

The more times that I set up my state of relaxation and confidence before I go into a presentation, the easier it becomes for me to access that state. In fact, I have done it so many times now that it is automatic for me.

Athletes do the same thing. Before they perform they imagine how they want their performance to be, they imagine being in the state that is most useful for them at the time, focussed, relaxed, excited, energised. Athletes talk all the time about being "in the moment". This is setting up a trigger using visual rehearsal.

The visual rehearsal sets up a neurological link for them so that when they get to the moment that they need to perform, this triggers an automatic response in them and they go into the state that they had imagined. It means that they can concentrate on the job at hand and they get the best results possible for them.

It is a simple and very powerful process that you can use for yourself:

- Think of an occasion in the future when you would normally go into a negative state. We will call this your unwanted state.
- Think about the sort of state that you would rather go into, one that is more useful to you. Name that state. We will call this your desired state.
- Now think of a specific time in the past when you can remember

going into that desired state.
- Go back to that time in the past when you experienced that desired state. See what you saw at the time, hear what you heard and really feel the feelings associated with that state.
- Again you may prefer to shut your eyes temporarily to do this.
- Now, think about the time in the future when you would like to experience that desired state. Just walk into that time in the future in your mind and see yourself experiencing your desired state. Notice how you look, notice what you can see, notice what you can hear, notice how you feel as you experience being in your desired state, just at the right time.

Congratulations, you have set up your neurological link. Now you need to rehearse the event again and again in your mind, each time associating with your desired state. Each time you rehearse you will strengthen the link and the trigger.

When the time comes notice how you feel. Notice that the feelings come automatically. Notice how good you feel.

Once you have been successful in this process, then you can use this technique for all sorts of different occasions in your life. Notice in your life where these triggers are already set up. Sights of things, sounds, the touch of something, smells and tastes all trigger different automatic thoughts. By noticing what is currently triggering your thoughts you can change the thoughts that are triggered so that they support you in the way that you want your life to be. This is how you will work towards getting your life the way that you want it.

Key Points

- We are motivated towards what we want and motivated away from what we do not want.
- Our saboteur is often behind motivations away from things that we do not want.
- It is important to identify which direction our motivation is

pointing us in so that we effectively manage our saboteur and get the results that we want in life.
- Use the tools provided to enable you to do that.

CHAPTER 13

Tuning up your motivation & energising your values

Stage 3 in Shaping your Future

Notice that a full memory or a full internal representation includes pictures, sounds, feelings, tastes and smells. When you are imagining future events then the most powerful, motivating internal representations will include most, if not all, of these sensory aspects.

When setting objectives and goals, in order to make them really compelling, then you can create an internal representation that includes pictures of what you will see, sounds, feelings, things that you may be touching, also smells and tastes.

Think back now to your values. Take your top value, look at what you wrote down alongside it in terms of why it is important to you. When you think of why it is important to you do you have a picture for that? Do you have an internal representation about how it looks, sounds and feels for you?

When I think of **progress** and achieving my potential I have a very specific picture associated with that in my mind. The picture is the one that I associate with achieving my potential. When I think about it I can see myself in the picture looking a certain way, I can see people around me, I can hear them, I can sense how I am feeling at the time. It feels great to me and it makes me feel good when I think about it.

Thinking about this is how I know that this value and the way that I have it set up in my thinking is empowering for me. I know that it is motivating for me and I know that it will stimulate me to produce positive results for me and for other people. This is because it is set up to motivate me towards what I want to happen.

If I had the value set up so that it was motivating me away from what I do not want to happen, then it would not be so great for me. If I wanted **progress** to move me away from procrastination, then I would be thinking about not procrastinating. Perversely this would necessitate that I think about procrastinating. It must do, mustn't it? I can't think about not procrastinating without thinking about procrastinating. My internal representation of "moving away from procrastinating" involves me procrastinating. I have a picture, with sounds and feelings associated with that internal representation. It is much less empowering and motivating for me to think this way. As I am thinking about something that I do not want, so I also get the negative emotions associated with that thing.

You can start to see now how the way that we hold the values in our head will determine our results. If we are less motivated to do something, then we are less likely to act.

In this way we need to make sure that our listed values have internal representations associated with them that direct our motivation towards what we want and not away from what we do not want. So we are going to start at the top and work our way down your values.

Take your top value first:

Step 1 - Assess your motivation

When you think about why your value is important to you:

- What picture do you get in your mind's eye?
- What internal representation do you get?
- Is it an internal representation of a future event that is towards what you want? Is it empowering for you?
- Does it motivate you when you hold the internal representation in mind?

If it is towards what you want and it motivates you then proceed to Step 3

Step 2 - Change the motivation direction to towards what you want

If it is away from what you do not want then we are going to change it around. Take some time now to think. How could you think about this value in a way that takes you towards what you would like more of in your life?

- Why else is this value important to you?
- What is another way of looking at the value that would motivate you towards getting a really positive outcome for you?
- What internal representation do you get around that?
- What are you seeing in your future, hearing and feeling?
- Does it feel good?
- Keep thinking of options until you find a way of thinking about it that makes you feel really positive.
- What we are searching for is a really clear picture of what you are doing when you are succeeding as a result of moving towards your value, when you are getting what you want.
- Have you got a new picture? Great.
- Go back to your list of values and scrub out your previous away-from motivation. Replace it with a description of this to-

wards motivation.

Step 3 - Giving your value the right level of motivation

So that your value is really motivating for you we just need to tweak some elements to your linked internal representation. Please recall your towards motivation picture now:

- Notice any people that may be around you. Really turn up the brightness on your picture so that it becomes crystal clear for you.
- Are there any sounds associated with your picture? Turn up the sounds
- How are you feeling as you get what you want? Really notice the great feelings that you get inside. Turn up the feelings so that they are just as you want them.
- Notice also when in time this is. How far into the future are you in your mind when you think of this success?
- Notice what you are going to have to do in order to bring about this reality.

Congratulations. You have successfully energised your value.

Take the next value on your list and go back to **Step 1 - Assess your motivation**. Work your way down to the bottom of your list.

When you have completed this process for each of your values on your list, then re-write your list so that it looks neat and tidy. Notice how you feel having all of the things that are important to you set up the way that you want them. This should give you a great sense of motivation and purpose.

This is the way that you are going to shape your future. You are deciding what you want more of in your life. You are giving yourself a purpose and a direction.

If you have any specific goals or objectives that you want to achieve in your life, then you can apply the same process.

Keep your values list to hand as you go about your day. Review and look over your list on a daily basis. This will ensure that you are communicating a message to your unconscious mind *this is what I want*. You are also communicating to your saboteur, you are keeping it at bay, reassuring it.

Notice when you are worrying. Notice that worry is merely a series of recurring negative internal representations. You know now that you can change your internal representations to how you want them. If you are worrying, then pay attention to the internal representations that you are creating. Notice that you can stop them. Think: how would I rather think? What is a way of looking at this that would be more useful to me? Notice that you can change your internal representations. Notice how much better that makes you feel. This is how you will change your worry habits.

Every time that you interrupt a series of negative internal representations and replace them with thoughts of what you want you are sending a message to your unconscious mind and to your saboteur. You are sending specific instructions over what you want. Your unconscious mind is there to serve you. You are forming new and empowering neurological links. The more frequently you think about what you want the more it will become automatic for you. Your unconscious mind will assist you in moving your life and shaping your life to the way that you want it.

Key Points

- The way that we portray things in our mind influences our mood and state of mind.
- We have provided you with a series of tools that you can use to improve your state of mind and get in a better mood instantly. This will enable you to get control of your state when you need to, overcome periods of anxiety and break that wor-

ry habit.
- We complete the process of shaping our life through our values by using some visualisation techniques. These techniques give us a sense of purpose, energise our values, give them the right motivation and ensure that they are working for us in the best possible way to enable us to live our lives the way that we want them. This will also help us in managing our saboteur.

Part 3 - **Your Mindfulness Programme**

CHAPTER 14

Mindfulness

It was a cool Saturday afternoon in the North of England, and I had been walking for two hours through the beautiful countryside. This was part of my weekend routine, a different walk every week. Sometimes in the hills, and sometimes through fields and over meadows. Sometimes I had company on my walk, though on this occasion I was walking alone. This was my chance to escape my work, my desk and emails, since the lure of my office in my spare bedroom was ever present when I was at home. I loved the feeling of freedom that I got whilst walking in the fresh air.

As I was walking along, all of a sudden I noticed something. I stopped. What was it? Something had just happened to me, like a light bulb coming on in my head. It was a definite shift in my attention. I could not quite pinpoint what it was. I started walking again.

Then it came to me. Almost straight away I stopped walking again. I realised what it was. I had just experienced silence. Everything inside was quiet. For the first time in a week I had stopped thinking. Those incessant thoughts of the week just gone and the week ahead had stopped and I had silence. It was beautiful. I was able to look out at the countryside and drink in the scene, I was able to hear the birds singing, the cool wind blowing through my hair. I could see the clouds whizzing by overhead, and smell the manure from the farmer's fields. I could really appreciate the true beauty of my surroundings for the first time during my two hour walk. It felt great to me, kind of familiar and yet strange at the same time. It felt like I was relaxing.

It dawned on me that this was the reason that I went walking every weekend. This was the only way that I managed to get this feeling of relaxation. It had taken two hours of walking this week to bring about this feeling. It was beginning to take longer and longer each week. *I must start planning longer walks*, I thought. The car was in sight. I began thinking about where I could go for a walk next weekend. The thinking restarted. I am sure that it did not stop again until the next weekend.

At the time I did not really appreciate what I had just experienced and how significant that it had been. It was only later that it finally clicked for me.

I resumed my habitual thinking patterns. There did not seem anything unusual to me in the way that I was thinking. It was how I was living my life at the time. I was *result focussed*, I was *goal oriented*. If I stopped constantly thinking, planning and reviewing then I was *taking my eye off the ball. Surely I would miss something that would be crucial to me in the week ahead?* Yet I found it hard to relax.

Hmmm. Thoughts of "missing something that would be crucial". What does that sound like to you? My saboteur? I was justifying my overthinking through fear of missing something that might be crucial if I stopped. That was definitely my saboteur at work, unconsciously fueling my overthinking. The thing was that it had become such a habit that it seemed quite normal to me, and anyway, I could not stop it even if I wanted to. I had become a servant to my mind.

This is something that I was doing at this point in time in my life and it is the kind of story that I hear regularly from people nowadays in my work. People say:

- I find it hard to wind down.
- I find it tricky to relax.
- I'm always thinking.
- I find it impossible to stop thinking about work.

These are the symptoms of an overworked and restless mind. It is a form of stress. It may not make you feel sufficiently ill to visit the doctor, as like me you may not even realise that there is a specific problem. In this way, millions of people live with it for years and years, it is like a hidden disease.

Over the next few chapters I am going to discuss with you some techniques that you can use in order to start keeping a quiet mind. I am going to remind you of how to rediscover your inner joy, how to make peace with your saboteur and how to find contentment.

Overthinking is an increasingly common problem in society. Is it any wonder? We live in the age of distraction. At any one time in our lives there are so many things demanding our attention, many of them brought about by the technology revolution.

I recently spent some time traveling on a train. Before the journey I was looking forward to shutting my eyes and resting. It had been a long day already. I arrived at the station ten minutes early and was pleased to see that the train had already arrived. It was commuter time, six pm. The train was already packed with business people ready to leave London on their daily 100+ mile journey home.

Fortunately I had reserved my seat, otherwise it was standing room only. I took my seat and started to settle in for the journey. I had a table seat, so I had three suited companions for my journey. I looked around to acknowledge them, they were not looking.

They seemed to be in a world of their own. The train started moving away from the platform and then the technology emerged....

I had a window seat on the left of the train. The gentleman on my right got his laptop out. The man directly in front of me pulled out his mini ipad and the chap to his left started tapping away on his phone.

There were children in the seats behind me. By the sound of it they were playing computer games.

I shut my eyes....and a phone started ringing. It sounded like a siren on a ship. Eeerrr, eeerrr, eeerrr. Really loud, the whole carriage could surely hear it. The man opposite who picked it up didn't seem to notice how loud it was, he had obviously heard it too many times. The man next to me put his headphones on.....and then attached them to his phone. He tapped on the screen a few times until he had found the contact that he was after.

The man opposite started talking more loudly, obviously signal was a problem. I could see his face getting flushed with frustration as he struggled to get his message across. He pulled the phone away from his head and stared at it. Connection lost. He puts it on the table. It rings again. Eeerrr, eeerrr, eeerrr.

So it went on for the next two hours. Meetings were arranged for early the next morning. Staff members were pulled away from their families to send various emails and do various pieces of work that obviously could not wait. Reports were written, emails sent and received, problems solved, for now.

The longer the journey went on the quieter the train eventually got. It might have had something to do with the various mini bottles of wine that were consumed around me. Headphones were removed from phones and plugged into laptops and ipads, the gaming commenced.

I watched and listened to all of this with fascination and a great deal of empathy.

This kind of scene is played out all over the western world every day. In airports, in waiting rooms, on trains, on buses and in homes. It is almost as though sitting and doing nothing in particular is not acceptable anymore. In workplaces, bosses demand 100% effort and put ever increasing demands on their staff. They know that they cannot insist on people skipping lunch but they encourage it. My boss never took a holiday, she hated it when I did. It was not a written rule that holidays were a luxury, but it was made known to me that this was the case. "How could they decide to take a holiday when we are behind target? They will be lucky to afford a holiday if they have not got a job!" These are the kinds of values that are pervading society.

When we are at work, then we are paid to work. We are encouraged to fit in more meetings, do more paperwork, work longer hours if required in order to do the work and meet ever increasing targets. In this way we are encouraged to eat lunch at our desks, we take no breaks. We take our work home with us to our families. This is why I describe it as a disease. It is a disease of expectation spread by society and it means that we become stressed and we find it very difficult to relax.

Over the following pages I am going to discuss with you how to get back your joie de vivre, your curiosity, your peace and contentment. I am going to share with you some techniques of mindfulness that you can use in your life to get back control over your wandering mind and so improve your level of happiness, well-being and relaxation.

These mindfulness techniques are time served techniques that are proven to be effective and beneficial in many ways. They have changed my life for the better and they have been proven over time consistently to work in reducing and eliminating stress, anxiety and depression.

One minute self reflection exercise.

Just take a minute to read the instructions below and then do the exercise:

1. Sit upright in your chair. It will be useful for your back to be self supporting and so a little away from the back of the chair. Have your feet flat on the floor. If you feel like it then close your eyes. Just place your hands in your lap or let them hang gently by your side.
2. Notice your breathing. Focus on your breath as the air flows in and out of your body. Notice any sensations in your body on each in-breath and on each out-breath. Just observe your breath, no need to change it in any way, we are not looking for anything to happen specifically.
3. As you are noticing your breathing and after a few moments your mind may wander off somewhere. When you notice this, gently bring your focus of attention back to your breath, without any self criticism. This very act of noticing that your mind has wandered and of regathering your attention without giving yourself a hard time is central to our mindfulness practice.
4. Eventually you may notice that your mind has become quiet and calm, the internal noise and chatter may die down. On the other hand, it may not. It is possible that you do notice a moment of tranquility and complete stillness, and it may be very short-lived. If you get a bit frustrated with yourself then this too may only be momentary. It does not matter what happens, just be aware of it and then let it be.
5. When you feel like it and after about a minute, open your eyes and bring your attention back into the room.

What did you find during this exercise? Were you able to concentrate on your breathing for long? Did you get interrupted by your thoughts? Did you notice any bodily sensations? Was there any self talk involved?

The first few times that I did this exercise I found that I had just got settled in the chair and I would think, *what was I supposed to be doing?* My mind had wandered already to other thoughts, even before I managed to start concentrating on my breathing.

In fact, even starting the exercise was a challenge. I would contemplate the instructions and think:

Yes, I can imagine how that might work. This is really interesting, I've understood that bit. Do I really need to actually do the exercise? I would rather move on to the next bit. I don't want to waste time here.

This was my mind resisting change, resisting something new. This was my saboteur reacting. "*I don't want to waste time here.*" - Fear of wasting time.

If you can remember noticing any resistance inside you to doing the exercise, then this may well have been true for you also. If you have read this far and you haven't done the exercise, then I encourage you to go back and do it. Let your saboteur know who is in charge.

If you managed to get all of the way through the exercise without any thoughts coming along and interrupting you, then that is fantastic. For most of us the actual act of noticing thoughts and letting them pass will have been the real test and the value that we received from the exercise.

Many people, noticing this for the first time are quite surprised at the lack of control that they seem to have over their thoughts. Our neocortex is conditioned to continually seek solutions. We notice a problem, and we solve it using our neocortex. This is a different kind of problem though because we cannot solve it by thinking about it. In fact, thinking about it is the problem.

For some people this can lead to us becoming frustrated with ourselves, we want to sit and concentrate on our breathing but we keep getting interrupted by thoughts. *Why can't I stop them? Why do they keep interrupting me? They are getting on my nerves.*

We are not used to such apparent disobedience. Our saboteur gets agitated.

Mindfulness is about observation of thoughts, it is about becoming fully present in our thinking. With mindfulness we learn to be compassionate with ourselves and this is how we will work with our saboteur to train it to operate to our advantage rather than to be obstructive for us.

Mindfulness is a skill, it is an art; and like any skill it will improve with practice. We are able to strike a balance between using our unconscious mind and our conscious mind whilst at the same time taming and befriending our saboteur.

Through mindfulness we are able to catch negative thoughts before the downward spiral begins. This is how we will achieve long-term improvement in our moods, in our feeling of well-being and in our happiness.

We are going to learn through mindfulness to be curious over our thoughts, not to take them personally and to treat unwanted thoughts, unhappiness and stress as clouds moving through our mind.

We are going to work on your mindfulness using a series of exercises. We are going to practise and review your exercises, this is how we will build your skills. We are going to give you the tools that you need to move through the learning cycle from unconscious incompetence, to unconscious competence.

The benefits of mindfulness are astonishing. As well as improved levels of happiness, reduced stress, reduced anxiety, feelings of well-being and peace, people have reported:

- Improved creativity and memory

- A reduction in blood pressure and hypertension
- Improved immune system, relieving people of chronic pain and cancer
- Improved relationships

Mind management through mindfulness

The great news for you is that you have already begun to gain a better understanding of what makes you tick. You have already begun to start shaping your future the way that you want it. Mindfulness will work in harmony with the tools that you have acquired so far during this book. We will expand your awareness further during this section to enable you to make better choices, create a better balance in your thinking, and this will help you change and improve your results in life.

We have learned how to use triggers in order to improve your mood in an instant. We have learned the role that memories play in your current state of mind, how creating memories for a better future can improve your motivation and guide your behaviour. We are going to concentrate in this section on creating an awareness of the present moment that will allow you to intercept negative thoughts before they start getting a hold. You will learn that your thoughts are not you, they are not real, and that with observation they evaporate in your mind. Just like clouds, if we observe our negative thoughts we can see them evaporate in our mind's eye, to be replaced with a void. In this void, we discover, exists our happiness, peace and serenity.

Through being mindful of the present moment we are able to get in touch with the purest sense of our experiences. We are able to discover our deletions, our distortions and our generalisations in our experiences. We will learn to observe our thoughts so that we can become further aware of the role that our judgements, our attitudes and our decisions play in cloaking our experiences.

So far we have experimented with planning and trawling through our memories and we are now going to explore how the mind is also aware. We can become aware of our thinking and we can become aware how we are thinking, in fact we are able to exist in the moment without the need to think at all.

Our conscious experience is not just made up of problem solving, planning and using logic. Our mind allows us access to our pure experience thus rediscovering our curiosity and excitement for every moment. We can observe our environment directly using our senses. We can hear the birds singing, see the flowers in all their beauty, smell the pollen, feel the earth beneath our feet, and savour the taste of the air around us.

At first this experience of pure existence may seem hard to come by. It did for me. Breaks in my incessant thinking were fleeting. After all, I had been conditioning my mind to work overtime for many years. Gradually, using the exercises that I will share with you, and with practice, the gaps in between thinking become longer and more frequent. We are able to gain objective distance from our thoughts, notice our bodily sensations. This brings mental clarity. We are conditioned to react to things immediately; these exercises teach us to be more patient, forgiving and compassionate with ourselves.

In a chaotic and distracting world, this is how you will discover some peace and serenity for yourself.

Victims of our own success

Carolyn appears to have it all. She is the commercial director of a very successful mid-sized company. She has a six figure salary, a lovely brand new, sparkling white four wheel drive car. She has a huge three bedroomed penthouse apartment that overlooks the sea. All the outward signs of success.

Carolyn's success has been hard earned. It has involved a great deal of sacrifice, all those weekends and evenings working towards her goals whilst everyone else has been out playing. Problem solving is her forte. Ultimately this is how she has achieved promotion after promotion to get her to where she is right now. If you want a job done and done properly, then give it to Carolyn. Her capacity for work seems limitless.

Yet, Carolyn is screaming inside. After a full weekend working she finally sits down on a Sunday evening to watch the sun set over the ocean from her balcony. Peace, and tranquility? Hardly. She cannot stop running and rerunning thoughts of the work that she has just completed. *Did I cover all of the angles? Did I miss anything? What is there that I am missing here?* Then thoughts of the week ahead creep in. *Four meetings in the morning. What do I need to prepare? Have I got all of my objectives clear in my head?*

The sun disappears without a single thought towards its beauty.

She finally finds a gap in her planning thoughts and reflects for an instant on her life. The loneliness, the lack of true fun, the increasingly frequent mood swings, the blackouts. It is twelve months since she had a holiday. This makes her feel miserable. She reverts to thinking about the week ahead. Better that than wallowing in self pity.

Society sees Carolyn as successful. She has achieved outward success at the expense of inner turmoil. This story is typical of those of high-flyers. It is like a form of self deception. One day they realise that business success is worth nothing without inner peace..and that is often where the problems start.

Being accustomed to achieving success wherever we lay our attention can cause us problems. Especially when the problem that we are seeking to solve is not solvable purely by directing our usual conscious thought processes towards it.

Carolyn chooses to ignore the inner problems rather than contemplate them. She has contemplated them before and has felt powerless to make any impact. This is not a usual result for her. She is a very skilled and intelligent lady. She outperforms all of her peers in IQ tests. Feeling powerless makes her feel uncomfortable, in fact it makes her annoyed. When she thinks of how powerless she is to solve her own inner problems, this makes her feel really frustrated and annoyed with herself.

Better to focus on something that can be solved, something that she can impact positively on. Deep down this frustration is tearing her apart. She can keep a lid on it most of the time but it is always there, bubbling under. Sometimes it erupts and someone cops it. *I must stop losing it with the staff. I don't seem to be able to. Grrr. It is so frustrating.*

This is how easy it is to become a victim of our own success. Society encourages us to be envious of people with money, with power and with celebrity. These things come with their own penalties. How much do we have to sacrifice in order to get them? How much recuperation time do we have to sacrifice? How much family time do we sacrifice? How much of our sanity do we give up in order to get what we want?

We set our sights on our goals and sometimes we get so involved with attaining our goals that we forget to look up and notice what is going on around us.

Mindfulness helps us to smell the roses of life, to step outside of our troubles and our goals, to liberate us. We learn to observe our emotions as a kind of background colour, mixing together our thoughts, feelings, bodily sensations and impulses and forming an overall mood or state of mind.

Mindfulness enables us to spot the participation of our inner critic, our saboteur, to recognise our fight or flight response. People say to themselves things like, "I should be happy". "What is up with me today?" We develop fears of the unknown, fears of failure, fears of success. We are coming to recognise these as our saboteur. Once we recognise and acknowledge our problems, they will disappear and lift like a mist on a spring morning. Once we recognise and acknowledge our saboteur it will remain peaceful, resting inside.

Being and Doing

We can achieve outer success by setting goals, deciding on outcomes and working tirelessly towards them. This can be rewarding in the short term but we can easily fall into the trap of failing to celebrate our success properly. We tend to replace old goals with new, more demanding ones, hardly taking the time to acknowledge how far we have come.

Goals and outcomes are only half of the story. They give us something to do. They put our mind into **doing mode**. Doing mode is where we solve our problems. We see a problem, and we focus on the gap. We see a goal and we recognise where we are at the moment. Our conscious mind then sets about working out what we have to do in order to close the gap. This is what we were doing when we were shaping our future earlier.

We each have an inbuilt acquisition strategy. We think, "Where am I now? Where do I want to be?" We notice the gap.

We think that if we worry enough then we will find a solution. The trouble is that we start missing the beauty around us. Think about the experience that I talked about earlier, whilst I was out walking in the countryside. My head was so consumed with reviewing and planning my work I walked for two hours without recognising the beauty of the world around me. Carolyn was able to sit through a beautiful sunset whilst looking out at sea, she missed it all because she was so wrapped up in her thoughts.

Our mind is brilliant at serving. If we give it problems, then it will use the doing mode to help us solve them. The more problems that we give it the better that it gets. The more complex the problems the more intricate and detailed the thinking, the more time that it takes to solve the problems.

Sometimes we need to step away from this doing mode, to just let the mind rest. Stress occurs when we do not rest our muscles and our brains. We rest our minds by becoming aware of our surroundings and what is going on inside. We rest our minds when we expand our awareness to just recognise this unique moment in time. This is the other half of the story, this is **being mode**.

Being mode allows us to observe as we would from the top of a mountain, gaining perspective. Being mode is pure awareness, it stops that pesky self talk.

The rain is lashing down. It is blowing a gale. People are scurrying across the street, struggling to keep their umbrellas from going inside out, wrapped up from the elements, scowling. The building opposite looks drenched and dreary. Other buildings are obscured by the pouring rain. The sky is invisible through the torrents descending. It is just a dark mess. I return to my computer to work on the next part of my project.

A few minutes later something catches my eye. What is that yellow light that I see outside? I grab a closer look. It is the sun reflecting off the building opposite. The building looks magnificent, mirrored glass shining brightly. Immaculate. I can see the blue sky and puffy white clouds reflecting off the glass now. Steam is rising off the top of the building. The sky beyond, limitless. I look down, people are meandering along the pavement, some are gathering to chat, smiling, faces relaxed.

It is incredible what a change of perspective can do. When we look at the world in a different light, then we gain new awareness. We see hope where once there was nothing, we see opportunity where once there were only problems. If we wait for the sun to come out, then we rely on outside influence to change our perspective for us. Mindfulness is something that we can do for ourselves to change our own perspective on reality. We can put ourselves in control of our own destiny by using mindfulness to shine a different light on our life.

We can gain awareness by looking at things in a different light, we can also look at things from a different place and from a different point in time. When we gain some kind of distance from our problems, then they seem to be less important to us. In fact, they can disappear altogether.

Think about how beneficial a holiday can be to an overworked mind. Most of us at some point in time have enjoyed a holiday so much that we do not want to return. Whilst we are away it is like living in a different world.

I remember vividly several holidays when on the first day there I could literally feel the stresses of life at work seeping out of my body as I began to relax on the beach. By the end of the holiday I couldn't remember what I was stressed about.

The build up to a holiday is normally frantic. Not only do we have to prepare for the holiday, sorting out, washing and ironing clothes to wear, making sure that we have all of our medicine, treatments and other paraphernalia. We also have to make sure that we clear the decks as much as possible at home. We attempt to tie up all our loose ends, preempting any possible scenarios at work and home that may occur and cause problems in our absence. This means that we actually have to put in an extra tough shift just before we leave. The night before the holiday, our mind is in serious doing mode.

Once we have set off, then we may be plagued by worries about those things that we did not quite manage to get done. We may be concerned about whether we locked the front door, whether we turned the gas off, whether we cancelled the milk delivery. The mind is still in doing mode.

Normally for me it was when I had arrived at the airport that things began to ease. There is nothing more that we can do at this stage about life at home. By the time that I arrived at our destination I was completely absorbed by all the new scenes in front of me, all the unfamiliar smells, sounds and hopefully the change in temperature! My mind switched to being mode. All of my brain's capacity for taking in bits of information was used up by taking in the new environment that I was in. I had not got space for the clutter of thoughts, anxieties and worries that I left at home. Somehow they did not seem important anymore anyway. It felt to me that I had been released from some kind of prison.

I observe this transformation in other people these days. For some people it takes longer for them to relax than it did for me. Recently I remember observing a middle-aged male holiday-maker from my sun lounger on a beach. He could not seem to sit down for five minutes. He would lie down with his phone in hand. Immediately, he would sit back up again. Then he would get up off his lounger and prowl about, up and down the beach. His body was so obviously tense, you could see it in his shoulders. I would look up again a couple of minutes later and he would be on the phone, barking instructions down the line. He would end the phone call and slam his phone down on the lounger, muttering to himself. Then the cycle would repeat itself. All this time his wife just lay passively on the lounger next to his. After a few episodes like this he would storm off, back to his hotel, leaving his wife to enjoy some peace and quiet while he no doubt went to do some work.

This continued for at least two or three days, although I could tell that the phone calls were getting less and less frequent. On the third day he even smiled! We returned to the same beach a few days later. I looked out for the holiday-maker and his wife. I could see his wife, on the same lounger. No sign of her husband. I assumed that he was working. Then I spotted someone in the sea playing with a luminous pink inflatable hoop. He was surfing in the waves as if he was a young child, laughing and joking with people around him. It was our man. No phone in sight. His transformation was complete.

We are going to use some mindfulness exercises to give you this altered perspective, to give you a different place from which to observe your thoughts. We are going to use the being mode to allow you a different way of knowing, so that you can better see how you are distorting reality. We will learn that we do not need to change the external environment to step outside of our conditioned mind and change the internal landscape.

Mindfulness is about paying attention on purpose, in the present moment, without judgement, to things as they actually are.

7 Traits of Doing and Being

Both doing and being modes are useful to us in different ways. In order for you to be easily able to identify your current mode of thinking you may like to consider a distinct shift between the doing mode and the being mode. They each have different traits:

1) Doing - Unconscious automatic pilot / Being - Conscious choices

Doing mode is home to our automatic pilot. When you are driving and not paying specific attention to what you are seeing, to your hand movements, to the changing of gears, then you are in doing mode.

Being mode is what you switch to once you realise that you are not paying attention. You become conscious of what actions that you need to take to turn left and right, to change up and down gears.

You are in doing mode when you are focussing on your goals without paying attention to where you are in the process, right now. In doing mode it is easy to be blind to options, to appear insensitive to others as you work towards your objectives.

In being mode you pay attention to your actions, to your feelings, to the world around you, to the actions and reactions of others.

In doing mode you are preoccupied with the past and the future.

In being mode, you are aware that you have a past and a future but you are living in the present moment.

2) Doing - Planning and Analysis / Being - Using your senses

When you are in doing mode you are constantly weighing things up in your mind. Thinking "what does this mean to me?" You are recalling memories and experiences to size up your experience and discover meaning. You are planning for the future and you are analysing the past.

In being mode you are absorbing the present moment through your senses. Using as much of your capacity for bits of information as possible to take in your experience through your senses.

Being mode is waking up to what is actually happening inside of you and in the world, moment by moment. This is how you discover how you are filtering the information, what you are distorting, deleting and generalising.

3) Doing - Judging and Comparing / Being - Accepting

In doing mode we apply our mind filters to make our judgements. We compare the real world with the way that we have it in our head. We are problem solving, we are looking at the gap between what we have and what we want. We are fighting with thoughts of how we can get things the way that we want them.

In being mode we accept the present moment for what it is. We gain distance from our judgements of what is good and what is bad. We accept the moment neutrally without placing judgement on it. As we suspend our judgement, so we find that this opens up our creative options. This is how we gain control of our life and deal with our problems.

4) Doing - We see our thoughts as real / Being - We treat our thoughts as mental events

We harbour our beliefs in doing mode. Our beliefs and our thoughts acquire a value for us in life. We hold our beliefs to be true for us. This includes beliefs about ourselves, our self image and our self worth. We mistake our interpretation of experiences and our thoughts for reality. In doing mode we fall into the trap of letting our thoughts become our master.

In being mode our thoughts are just events in the mind. We realise that our thoughts are not us. They are nothing but imagined events, clouds that soon pass by. In this way we learn to become the master over our mind, the servant.

5) Doing - Fight or Flight / Being - Approaching

Our saboteur lives in our doing mode. Doing mode is where we experience avoidance. We have goals that we move towards and we have goals that we move away from. Often in doing mode we move away from things because it is instinctual. In doing mode our saboteur has influence and control.

We learn that once we approach our fears, once we approach our problems, they disappear before our eyes. In being mode we are compassionate towards ourselves and our problems, we take a friendly approach. We become curious of the things that we feel like avoiding, we discover our saboteur, we turn towards our negative feelings. Eventually the saboteur becomes restful, peaceful. Our negative feelings dissipate.

6) Doing - Surfing time / Being - Present

In doing mode we are preoccupied by traveling back into the past and into the future. Our moods and state of mind become determined by the memories from our past and thoughts of the future.

See your thoughts as they occur in being mode, see memories as memories, see planning as planning. This allows us to experience life as it is right now rather than experiencing extra pain through surfing back and forward in time.

7) Doing - Withdrawals / Being - Deposits

Imagine your life in terms of an energy savings account. When we exercise, when we sleep peacefully, when we eat the right things, when we rest, then we make deposits into our energy savings account. When we go out partying, when we work too hard, when we fail to look after ourselves, then we make withdrawals from our energy savings account. Life is about creating a balance.

When we spend too much time in doing mode, then we are making too many withdrawals. We are focussing so hard on our goals that we forget to take exercise and to look after our relationships. Eventually this will cause problems for us, we are depleting our reserves of energy and integrity. At first it is easy to see these withdrawals as temporary, but as we know thinking is habitual. After a time we will start to feel exhausted, drained, sapped of energy and listless.

Being mode restores our balance. As we start paying attention to our well-being, health and relationships with loved ones, so we make deposits in our reserves of energy and integrity. We get back the sparkle in our eyes and the spring in our step.

Through the following mindfulness exercises you will begin to notice these seven traits in your mode of thinking. You will begin to notice when you are over-thinking, over-planning and over-analysing. Your mindfulness will provide you with some alarm bells for you to recognise as you go about your day. It will assist you in restoring balance to your thinking.

You will notice that a shift in respect to any one of the doing and being traits will shift your whole mode of thinking. As you spend more time in being mode you will grow your curiosity, you will treat yourself with warmth and you will become more accepting of others. You will receive and accept life as it is, become more fulfilled and worry free. Mindfulness gives you a sense of what is important and what is not, a sense of perspective.

You are going to need to devote some time to these exercises. Mindfulness is a skill, and with practice you will improve and refine your skills. As you do this you will notice the improvements in your life.

The benefits of mindfulness are incremental. The more you practise the better will be your results. At the same time you can gain results and changes in your brain in almost an instant. Neurological networks react to changes immediately and in this way, even after a ten minute exercise you will be firing new electrical connections through your neurons and transmitting new levels of chemicals, thus adjusting the chemical balance in your brain and in your body. You can expect to feel differently as a result. Once you start planting the seeds, then you encourage happiness to take root.

Expanded Awareness - 1 minute exercise

First read the instructions to rehearse the exercise visually. Then carry out the steps below:

1) From a seated position choose a spot on a wall to look at. It could be a small mark or part of a pattern, something like that. Make sure that the spot is clearly visible and is just above the height of your head.
2) Look straight ahead at the wall and then without moving your head, raise your eyes to look at the spot.
3) Look at the spot for a few moments. Notice how, as you start to relax your eyes from the edges, so your vision expands across the whole wall.
4) Still looking at the spot, notice how you can see the whole of the wall, right to the corners. You will see the corners of the room in your peripheral vision.
5) As you continue to relax your eyes and look at the spot, notice now that you can see the ceiling and floor as well as the corners of the room. Your awareness is expanding.
6) Continue to look at the spot and you will be able to pull your awareness around you further, so that you are seeing

almost 180 degrees using your peripheral vision.
7) Without taking your gaze off the spot you can make out various things in your peripheral vision: colours, shapes, objects.
8) At this stage see if you can expand your awareness further, so that you are encompassing things to your side and around the back of you.
9) Notice the sounds around you and things that you see. Notice how you feel as you remain in this state of expanded awareness for a minute or so.

How did that go? Did you notice your awareness expanding?

Sally did this for the first time and remarked on how amazed that she was by how much she could see. She said, "I was looking at a spot on the side wall in my living room. I was quickly able to notice the whole wall in my peripheral vision. The edges were a bit blurred, but I could definitely see the corners of the room. As I continued to observe, I noticed that I could make out various objects in my peripheral vision. I could see our window at the front of the house and through the window I saw a blue van driving past.

As I continued to pay attention, I began to notice how calm I felt. I found it a very relaxing and curious experience."

Other people have noted how the internal chatter appears to stop, the self talk ceases. People have remarked that it feels a bit like being in a light trance but remaining very alert.

The key to the exercise is that by providing instruction and requiring an expanded awareness, so we begin to monopolise the bits of information that we are processing in our brain. The whole of the capacity for processing information becomes used up in taking in information through our senses and through following the instructions. There is no remaining capacity for worries, anxieties, planning, judging or self talk. We shifted our attention to being mode.

The more people practise this exercise, the more they get comfortable in remaining in this state of expanded awareness. In fact after a few goes people often feel confident enough to shift their gaze away from the spot on the wall, and move their head around, whilst staying in the state and maintaining their awareness.

You may find, as you do this, that after a short while you lose concentration. This is quite normal. You may find that you forget what you were doing. Also, thoughts of what you did earlier and what you are planning to do later send you off track. This is our doing mode wrestling back control.

Potato Crisp exercise

It is important for this exercise that you choose a flavour of crisp that you have never tried before, or one that you have not eaten recently. Here goes:

- Open the packet. What can you smell? Let the smell wash over your senses.
- Take out a single crisp. Hold it in your hand and examine it. Look at the detail of the shape. Is it straight or curved? Are the edges rounded or sharp? Can you see anything on the surface? Any flavouring or salt? Does the surface glisten or is it dull? Notice what colours you can see.
- Put it into your mouth. Resist the temptation to bite into it at this stage. See if it is possible to let it rest on your tongue. How does it feel resting on your tongue? Does it start softening as it mixes with your saliva? What flavours can you taste?
- If you notice your mind wandering as you do this, then just pay attention to that happening and gently bring your thoughts back to the crisp in your mouth.
- When the crisp has softened a little bit, then bite into it with your teeth and notice how it breaks apart. How does it sound

> as it breaks? Chew it. Let it mix with your saliva. Notice the tastes now.
> - Swallow the crisp when it is broken down sufficiently. Notice how it slides down your throat.
> - Repeat this with the next crisp.

How was that for you? Was the experience different from normal? How was it different to just popping a crisp in your mouth and eating it without paying attention?

Mindfulness Mind Management Programme

The exercises so far have given you a taster for the programme to come. We are going to provide you with a number of further exercises that are designed to work together in expanding your awareness of how you are thinking, addressing each of the seven traits of doing and being modes of thinking.

The exercises are designed to be followed in sequence so that we gradually build your skills and open up your awareness to the set of mind management tools that are already well within your grasp.

The various sections of our mindfulness programme generally consists of several parts:

- Mindfulness exercises
- Exercise summary
- Exercise review
- Habit breakers

The exercises are designed for you to take some quiet time to explore how you are constructing your reality and to enable you to get to know yourself better. We will provide you with some really practical ways to see your thoughts.

The habit breakers compliment the exercises and will re-ignite your curiosity, taking you out of autopilot and bringing your awareness into the world around you.

Both the exercises and the habit breakers are going to take some time. You will not find the time, so you will need to make time. You will need to get familiar with the exercises to really experience the full benefits, so plan to do each one several times before moving on to the next one. I suggest putting some time in your diary to complete them. Make some appointments, meetings with yourself either in the early mornings, or evenings and commit to keeping them. Consider this your daily practice. For the exercises, you will need to find somewhere peaceful and comfortable. Somewhere that you can be sure of not being disturbed.

People report that in the long run this programme actually saves time rather than using it up.

Think about the amount of time that you are currently wasting thinking about past events, running and rerunning them over in your mind. Think about the amount of time that you are wasting worrying about events that may never happen in the future.

How much time are you actually spending currently living in this moment in time?

When I first considered this question I was shocked to realise that I probably was spending less than 5% of the time actually living for this moment. Past and future thinking creeps up on us. I was completely unaware how much of my life was passing me by without me noticing and appreciating it.

At the time I was not aware that I was not happy. I thought that I was. However, I now recognise that it was a false sense of happiness based on a mind created world rather than true joy and contentment that can be experienced by purely paying attention to our current state of being and being curious to discover the delights of the world around us.

You will not always be successful in your practice. It is a good idea to prepare yourself now for feelings of failure. Success is always achieved after a number of unsuccessful episodes. It takes time to become a master of anything, but with perseverance you will get there. The only failure is failure to take any action at all. Your saboteur will try to tell you otherwise of course.

Key Points

- We live in a world full of distractions, and overthinking has become an increasingly common problem. Technology places constant demands on our attention, and we are losing the ability to relax.
- Mindfulness enables us to become aware of our thinking, it provides us with a break from the stress of overthinking. We are able to watch and observe our thoughts, we see them as clouds and as we watch them they disperse in front of us.
- Mindfulness is about being in the present moment in our minds and bodies. As we develop presence of mind so it allows us distance from our thoughts and we become aware of how we are distorting our reality, the judgements that we are making and the role that our decisions and attitudes play in cloaking our experiences. We are able to exist in the moment without any need to think at all. This is how we achieve peace and serenity.
- The world teaches us that success is wealth: having a nice house, a nice car. But sometimes this outer success comes at the expense of our inner peace. We learn to solve problems using our conscious thought processes but these processes are often the cause of our inner problems, not the solution. Mindfulness helps us to work on our inner success as in the end this is the only success that matters.
- There are two modes of operating in our minds: doing and being.
- Doing mode is planning, reviewing, judging, problem solving.
- Being mode is using our senses to experience the world

around us and becoming aware of what is going on internally in our bodies. Being mode gives us distance from our thinking, which allows us to take a different perspective on our problems.
- Expanded Awareness Exercise - we use our peripheral vision to monopolise our attention. This has the impact of eliminating self talk and taking us into being mode.
- Potato Crisp Exercise - This mindful eating experience helps us to realise that we often eat on autopilot. By paying focussed attention to eating we are able to magnify the sensory experience and pleasures in eating, pleasures that are gained from having presence of mind. This demonstrates just how much of our experiences we normally miss due to our attention being elsewhere.
- Prepare for the mindfulness programme ahead by making time every day for your practice.

CHAPTER 15

Getting to know your autopilots

"I'm home!" John calls out as he locks the front door behind him. No reply.

Aahhh, a bit of time to myself. What a week! I need some wine, quickly.

John trudges upstairs to get changed, conversations from the day's meetings resurfacing in his thoughts. It went really well with his boss today, she seemed really pleased with the project that he had just finished and it looks like the company will be implementing his suggestions. It is going to mean a busy period ahead for him, starting with the meeting with his team first thing on Monday morning.

Oh, crikey, I haven't managed to firm up the meeting room. What are my options?

John starts running through his options in his head.

The hotels will be open over the weekend, although the corporate booking service will probably be closed. Maybe they will be able to access the system from the front desk. I could always put down a deposit using my own card if necessary. My card! Arrgh, I need to phone the card company to order a new one, I had trouble using it the other day, I think that the magnetic strip must be damaged. Anyway, what other solutions are there?

John ponders further solutions as he is changing his clothes. He notices his phone flashing out of the corner of his eye.

I must have forgotten to switch the volume back on. Missed call. It was Susan (wife), I wonder what she is up to? In fact there are seven missed calls! One from Susan and six from Alison (boss). Oh no. What have I done wrong? Just when I was starting to relax as well.

He switches the phone volume back on and immediately it starts ringing. It is Susan again.

"Hello."

"Where are you?" Susan asks.

"I'm at home. Just got in. Where are you?" *Shopping again, no doubt.*

"I'm at your Mum and Dad's. We are ready to go."

Ready to go? Oh noooo.

It dawned on John that he had agreed to meet his wife at his Mum and Dad's house, straight from work to save time. They were due to set off from there to see their son in his school play.

John had been so preoccupied with thoughts driven by his autopilot, that he had completely forgotten about their arrangement.

The unconscious mind picks up trains of thought, like conversations that we have had during our day, and it sets off various series of thoughts around the conversations. Did we say the right thing? Did we get what we were looking for from the conversation? Should we have said something else? How did it make us feel?

It then picks up other trains of thought triggered by the original thoughts. We set off on a tangent. We receive another series of thoughts around that subject. All of this is happening on autopilot. As we think these thoughts we become submerged in them. The actions that we are taking as we have these thoughts are unrelated to the thoughts themselves. They take place using their own series of behavioural autopilots.

Driving a car is a perfect opportunity for our mind to work on autopilot. We are able to steer, change gear, brake and accelerate, and navigate the traffic all without conscious thought. I used to have a four hour drive home some evenings from work. I could go almost the whole journey without actually paying conscious attention to the physical act of driving. It was normally only a sudden act of braking from the car in front on the motorway that would wake me from my reverie.

One Friday evening after an unremarkable day at the office I drove home in my own little world of thoughts. I parked up and was about to get out of the car, when I noticed that I had driven onto the driveway of a house that I lived in ten years previously. It was the first time that I had been back to that house since I left it all of those years ago. It was five miles away from where I now lived. My unconscious mind had guided me home, to my old address!

It does not matter how good you think that you are at doing more than one thing at once, you have a limited number of bits and chunks of information that you can process at any one time in your brain. Once you have used up your seven plus or minus two chunks, then there is no further capacity. This is when the autopilots take over and this is when habits arrive.

If we are preoccupied with thoughts or worries and we are constantly running and rerunning thoughts of events in the past and worries about predicted events in the future, then it is quite possible that this process uses up nearly all of our seven plus or minus two chunks. We have no further capacity for conscious processing, and so our automatic unconscious processes take over. The problem there is that the unconscious mind needs clear instructions to follow, like a small child. In the absence of clear instructions from our conscious mind it runs free, and is influenced by our saboteur. This is when we tend to get unwanted behaviours.

Think of how the Windows operating system works on a computer. With a few windows open the computer runs smoothly. The more applications that we open, the more windows that we have open, the slower the processing of information becomes as the computer takes time to catch up with instruction. Eventually, the computer may freeze and shut down.

Our central processing unit of a brain has a limited capacity. Whenever we go over that capacity we start experiencing symptoms and feelings of distraction, overwhelm and confusion. Habits trigger thoughts. Thoughts trigger more thoughts. We can spend hour upon hour recycling these thoughts without actually paying conscious attention to what we are thinking. We become overloaded, frustrated, we lose our energy and are taken over by exhaustion.

The aim of this module is to allow you to start noticing when your autopilot is switched on. We are going to do a couple of exercises that will help you identify when you are running your automatic thought patterns and when you are generating automatic behaviours. As opposed to when you are making conscious choices and paying attention to the present moment.

Chocolate Exercise

This is similar to the Potato Crisp exercise that we did earlier. We extend the exercise a little to bring further mindfulness to your conscious attention.

Choose a type of chocolate that is less familiar to you, one that you haven't had for a while. You will need to set ten minutes aside to do the exercise. Switch off all of your technology. Choose somewhere quiet, where you are able to remain undisturbed for the duration of the exercise.

Read the exercise through first of all so that you are prepared for each step. You will need a pen and a piece of paper to record your thoughts after you have completed the exercise.

We are going to ask you to eat the chocolate in a mindful way, paying attention to the various stages involved in the act of eating. We would recommend that you spend about twenty seconds on each of the following stages:

1) Holding

Choose a single piece of chocolate. Pick it up and hold it between your fingers and thumb. Get really curious. Notice which hand you choose to pick it up with. Which parts of the chocolate piece are you touching? An edge, a side, the top, the bottom? Notice the weight of it.

2) Seeing

Really get a close look at it. Imagine that you are looking at chocolate for the first time. Can you see different colours in it? Are there any machine made markings on the piece? Is it smooth or are there bumps in it? Swivel your hand around a bit so that you get a good look at it from various angles. Notice where the light is shining on the surface. Are there any shadows being created?

3) Touching

Gently move the chocolate around using your fingers. Can you feel the texture? How does it feel? Notice the difference in feel between any edges and the sides.

4) Smelling

Bring the chocolate up to just underneath your nose. Breathe in gently through your nose. What can you smell? Let the smell fill your awareness. What sensations does that bring about?

5) Tasting

Place the piece of chocolate on your tongue. Notice as you do this how your arm and hand know exactly what movements are required. Notice also that your tongue knows just how to receive it, naturally. Without chewing, use your tongue and the roof of your mouth to explore it. What are you tasting? Chocolate typically has over 300 different flavours. What different flavours are you noticing? Continue to experience this for thirty seconds or more. Notice when the chocolate starts melting. Does this change the flavour in any way? Does it release further flavours?

6) Swallowing

As the chocolate continues to melt, notice as the physical shape gradually disintegrates. Do not swallow just yet. Notice as the intention to swallow arises. Observe the thought. See it as a thought and bring full awareness to it. Notice how your tongue prepares to participate in the act of swallowing.

Swallow the chocolate now. Do it deliberately, slowly. Notice as it slides down your throat. Where can you feel it going from there? What sensations do you get? Any new flavours? Notice what happens to your tongue after you have swallowed.

7) Aftertaste & Sensations

Notice the aftertaste in your mouth. What are the remaining tastes? How does your mouth feel? Are there any remnants of

> the chocolate still in your mouth? What sensations are there? How does your tongue feel? How about any other after-effects? Swallow any remaining chocolate. Notice how that feels and tastes. Do you have an inclination to have a second piece?
>
> Take your pen and piece of paper and write some notes on your experience. You may like to use the headings above to note what you saw, felt, smelt, tasted and any sensations that you had. What did you notice about your thoughts?

Fiona wrote that "it was like a whole new eating experience." She found that the smells were "almost overwhelming. I loved the smell of chocolate anyway, but I had never experienced it as being quite as powerful as that before."

Geoff explained, "My mouth started watering as I read the instructions. As I held it I really wanted to just pop it in my mouth and chew it. I am glad now that I didn't."

Paul said,"I have to say that I felt a bit silly at first... At the end I realised how little attention I normally give to what I eat."

Like many of our everyday activities, we tend to take eating food for granted. How often do we really pay attention to what we are eating? How many of the processes involved with eating do we do automatically? How often do we take the time to really appreciate the smells and tastes of our food? What are we normally thinking about when we are eating?

We tend to eat what we know that we like and avoid food that we dislike, but how often do we really pay attention to the full eating experience?

Many of us eat at our desks, writing and replying to emails. We eat in front of the TV. We eat while we are in conversation with other people. How much of our attention is actually on the plea-

sure of eating, the aromas of our food, how it makes us feel?
Did you notice any saboteur involvement in taking the time to follow the exercise through and paying full attention? Your saboteur will normally react to this in some way. It is something that is unfamiliar to you and your saboteur will attempt to preserve the old habits. This is likely to be why Paul felt "silly" and Geoff felt like he wanted go ahead and start chewing the chocolate straight away.

As you start to pay full attention to things in the present moment, you can see now how much of your experience has been lost in the past, how much pleasure you have missed out on over the years. Just think of how much pleasure you have been missing by not seeing, hearing, touching, feeling, tasting and smelling things as you go about your day. Let your saboteur ponder this. How much of life is just passing you by as you fail to pay attention to the moment at hand? There is no other time in life that matters, now is all that is important. Your time is now. Enjoy the present moment, live it, breathe it, drink it in.

Routine everyday activities and our autopilots - Exercise

Eating is just one of our everyday activities that is usually carried out on automatic pilot. You can probably think of many more but we have listed below a number of activities where you can now practise applying mindfulness:

- Showering
- Brushing your teeth
- Walking to work, or to catch public transport
- Driving
- Sitting on public transport
- Making a cup of tea or coffee
- Washing up
- Ironing

Pick an activity that you would like to experiment with. Repetition is key to building your awareness and skills, so once you have chosen your activity then you need to commit to repeating this exercise every day for a week.

When it is time to do your activity, place all of your awareness on the activity itself. This does not necessarily involve slowing down the process. Do it as normal and be acutely aware as you are doing it of all of your actions and how you are experiencing the activity. Observe your thoughts. Notice if and when you get distracted. Bring your attention back to the activity at hand.

Showering - As you step under the shower notice any sensations in your body. Can you hear the water hitting your skin, splashing on the floor of the shower? Can you feel any differences in temperature in different parts of the shower? Can you see any fine mist appearing in the shower? Any coming off your body? Can you feel the pressure of the shower as the water meets your skin? Pay attention to your hand movements, notice how precise they are in cleaning the different parts of your body. If you use soap, notice the sensations of the bubbles on your skin. Is there a scent from the soap? Does your skin smell differently?

If you catch your mind drifting off, then pay attention to the thoughts that you are having and just watch them gently fade away as you observe them. Go back to paying attention to your experience in the moment.

Brushing your teeth - Notice where your thoughts are as you start brushing. Can you taste the toothpaste? What sensations are there in your mouth? Pay attention to the movements of your hand and fingers as you brush. Can you feel the brush on your teeth? What is happening with your tongue?

Walking - Pay attention to the feel of the floor under your feet. Notice the temperature of the air around you. What can you hear? Can you hear your own footsteps, your clothes rustling? What can you smell? Notice how you are co-ordinating your

> movements, one foot in front of the other. Are your arms moving? What are you thinking about as you walk? If your experience gets disturbed by thoughts of the past and future, then notice this, congratulate yourself on your discovery. Let these thoughts go and return to your senses.

When I first did the chocolate exercise I began to realise how much of my actual experience in life I was missing. It dawned on me that I was largely ignoring my sensory experiences, living in my thoughts. It was like a whole new world opened up to me. I had been unconsciously blocking recognition of the world around me, the sensations and feelings in my body. The amazing thing to me was that despite the fact that I had been doing this, I did not lose the ability to begin experiencing, recognising and enjoying these things when I became deliberately mindful. I realised that I retained my natural ability to become acutely aware of what I was seeing, hearing, feeling, tasting and smelling. I just needed to switch my attention to these things. It was going to take practice but the awareness that I had the power to choose was liberating for me.

Chloe experienced it slightly differently. She said that she struggled to stay focussed on the exercise itself as she was plagued by all of her thoughts. Whenever she tried to clear them in order to experience the present moment they just kept on reappearing. "I got really frustrated with myself. I couldn't seem to clear my mind. Thoughts just kept on getting in the way."

This is quite common and it is still a step forward. We get our first glimpse of clear daylight in between our thoughts. We realise how much thinking we are actually doing and our conscious mind starts looking at the gap between where we are and where we want to be. We decide we want more daylight. Our mind then goes off in search of a solution. This starts the doing mode of thinking. We are back in our thoughts. We notice this, it provokes our reptilian brain fight or flight response, our saboteur stirs into life and we get frustrated with ourselves.

As frustrating as it may seem, we have to understand that we have been conditioning these automated thinking patterns for many years. They will not disappear over night. We need to re-condition our systems, generate new habits and new triggers, we will do this through practising the exercises in this programme.

Mindfulness encourages us to observe the patterns of thinking rather than resist them. Rather than trying to switch off the mind, we acknowledge it, we notice what is going on. Over time we will begin to approach our thoughts rather than moving away from them or rejecting them. The act of doing this improves our awareness, settles our saboteur, gives us more choices and options. Thus enabling us to gain greater control of the mind and make better decisions for our life.

This is a two stage process. First, we need to become aware of our doing mode of thinking. We need to observe our thoughts passively. Notice what the thoughts are and where they are taking us. Second, we must develop methods for dissolving the habits that monopolise our thinking and drive routine behaviour. We are going to give you the tools to do both of these things.

You need to experience this for yourself. It does not matter how many times we tell you that this works. You can even read this and believe us, but you will not know it to be the case unless you actually discover it for yourself through practice.

Key Points

- Thinking often takes place unconsciously.
- We experience chains of thoughts that seem to come out of nowhere and are not linked to what we are doing at the time. Many of these thoughts are repetitive and unwanted. Meanwhile we operate our behaviours on autopilot.
- Confusion, overwhelm and distraction occur as a result of us overthinking and trying to process too many bits of informa-

tion.
- Chocolate Exercise - Helps us to identify how we run our autopilots. Start noticing that you can watch your thoughts and you can use all of your senses to gain mindfulness of your experience.
- Use everyday activities such as walking, washing up, showering, brushing teeth as a trigger to practise being in the moment, notice your thoughts interrupting you and become acutely aware of your pure sensory experience.

CHAPTER 16

Body and Breath

We are about to get ready for your first full mindfulness exercise. Let's call these exercises your me-time mindfulness exercises.

In this exercise we are going to reacquaint you fully with your body and your breath. We are going to use your breath as a focus for your attention and we are going to explore how it relates to the sensations in your body.

In a previous section we explored how you can trigger certain thoughts and change your mood by bringing back memories of previously experienced events. In the same way we are going to use this experience of becoming aware of your breathing in order to help us to set up triggers to allow you to become more aware of your doing and being modes. Over time and with practice this will allow you to enter and spend time in being mode by just remembering to observe your breathing.

There are several benefits of using the breath as an anchor to enter being mode:

1) Breathing happens naturally, we do not need to think about

breathing to get it to happen. This helps us to relax any belief that we may have around the need to be in control. When we notice the breath, even for short periods, then we relent on our need to fix things. We can just pay attention to the breath.

2) Whenever we pay attention to our breathing it will be there. It is ever present. At any time we can choose to pay conscious attention to our breathing. We do not usually notice it, we take it for granted and it is an automatic process but if we choose to notice it, then it will be there. In this way, once we have set up noticing our breathing as a trigger for mindful thoughts, for being mode, then we can use the anchor at any time and enter that state immediately. If we are in a particularly frustrated or stressed state, or any other state that is not useful for us, then we can pay attention to our breathing and enter a more relaxed and mindful state straight away.

3) Breathing is a great way to gage our feelings. By noticing whether our breathing is shallow, deep, rough, smooth, long or short we can start to discover what is going on inside.

4) Breathing grounds us in the here and now. When we notice our breathing then we must be in being mode, in the here and now. We can't breathe in the past or future, can we?

Your "Me-Time" Exercises

I would encourage you to set aside some time six days a week in order to do one of these me-time exercises. Start with this first exercise and repeat it every day for a week. Then move on to the next me-time exercise, do that every day for a week and so on.

It is important that you practise the exercises on a regular basis. You will probably notice some change as a result of just doing the exercise once, but do not worry if you do not, it will come. We are developing a habit and a skill and like most skills, and all habits this takes time for it to sink into our system.

Doing each exercise several times before moving on to the next one ensures that you get familiar with the process of the exercise. You will find that what you have learned grows with familiarity. Do not expect that everything will go perfectly for you on the first run through. You will discover that there will be some things that need practice in order for you to perfect them. The more practice that you do the more that you will learn about yourself and about the process. The more times that you do the exercise and connect with your breathing, the stronger that the anchor will be for you.

Life is unpredictable, so if you have to miss a few days of practice, then don't worry, just pick it up again as soon as you can. When you resume, then go back to the exercise that you were doing before you had your break, practise that exercise again for a week and then move on to the next one.

Breath and body exercise - Me-Time Exercise 1 (10 Minutes)

Before you start make sure that you are not going to be disturbed for the next ten to fifteen minutes. This means turning off any technology that might interrupt you, for example your phone. Pick a room where you can sit comfortably or lie down with no interference from other people. Most people find that they can relax most comfortably by lying down.

Have a good read through the instructions before you start. As you read them, imagine yourself doing the exercise, this visualisation will prepare you for the exercise ahead.

Do not be too concerned with the minutiae of the instructions. The spirit in which you approach these exercises is much more important than precision in following all of the steps. After you have completed the exercise you can review how the experience was for you and compare it with the instructions, ready for the next time.

Preparation

1) Get comfortable in your position, either lying down or sitting. If your legs are crossed, then uncross them. Have your arms out by your side and uncrossed. If possible open up your hands and have the palms facing upwards. You may find that it is most relaxing to do the exercise with your eyes closed. If you wish to keep your eyes open then lower your gaze. You are ready to begin.

Awareness of the body

2) Bring your attention to your body. Notice what you are touching with the various parts of your body. If you are lying down, then notice which parts of your body are in contact with the surface that you are lying on. Notice one at a time if your arms, your legs, your feet, your back, your head are touching the surface. If you are sitting, then notice your feet touching the floor, your legs on the chair, any other part of your body resting against the chair.

Notice how the surface you are resting on feels through each part of your body. Is it soft or hard, warm or cool? What sensations are you getting in the various parts of the body as they touch the surface?

3) Imagine that you are shining a light on your body. This is the light of your awareness, your 'spotlight of attention'. Focus in your spotlight of attention to your feet. Focus it now right down to your toes. Go right to the end of your toes and focus on the very end of your toes. What sensations are there at the end of your toes?

Start to expand your spotlight a little bit so that your attention expands to the soles of your feet, your heels and moving out to include the tops of your feet and your toes. Notice, moment to moment, all and any sensations that you get in your feet. Spend a few moments here. Pay attention to any sensations that you become aware of and notice that they come and go. Notice as they appear and dissolve of their own accord. (As you read these instructions, you may be able to notice these sensations coming and going right now.) If you do not become aware of any sensations, then do not worry, this is fine. The aim is not to generate sensations, just to observe them as they fizzle in and out.

4) Gradually expand your spotlight of attention further to include your legs. Moving the spotlight up your legs to include your knees and then the whole of both legs. Bit by bit let your spotlight move out so that it includes your whole body, moving up from the legs through your pelvis, hips, stomach, and chest, up to your shoulders. Let it continue to expand out to include your arms, your neck and your head.

5) Spend a couple of minutes letting your attention gently rest on the whole of your body. Notice any sensations that are there. Just pay attention to your body without trying to fix anything. Get curious in your observation and just enjoy letting your body be as you find it. This is passive observation, this is attention to the moment to moment changes in your body.

Awareness of your breath

6) Now bring your attention to your breathing. Notice as you breathe in and out. As you breathe in notice any movement in your stomach, any sensations in your stomach as the air fills your lungs. As you breathe out continue to pay attention to your stomach as the air empties from your lungs. You can place your hand gently onto your stomach if you like to feel the movement.

7) As you continue to breathe in and out notice the air going into your body, follow it down into your lungs and seemingly down into your stomach. As you breathe out follow the movement of the air up through your lungs and out of your

body.

8) Notice any sensations in your body as you breathe in and out. Do you get any sensations as the different parts of your body expand and contract with your breathing? Are there any slight pauses between breaths? Follow any moment to moment changes in your body as you continue to breathe.

9) Just breathe in and out naturally. If you feel a tendency to alter your breathing in any way, then just notice this thought and let it be.

Continue to keep your awareness on the breath and the sensations in your body for eight minutes or so.

Notes on interrupting thoughts and mind wandering

As you carry out this exercise you will inevitably find that you are interrupted by some form of mind wandering. This is your habitual thinking kicking in. This is doing mode interrupting you.

You may get images, sounds, feelings, worries, thoughts, anxieties, or any kind of day-dreaming activities distracting you from the exercise. This is quite normal. If you do notice this, then congratulate yourself as you have noticed this by being mindful! Purely by noticing that your mind has wandered you have taken a step forward. If and when this happens then just gently bring your awareness back to your breath and continue from where you left off.

As your awareness is on your body and your breathing, so you are in being mode, you are in the moment, in the now. When you are distracted you are pulled off into doing mode, into the past or the future. When you notice this happening, then you notice it from the now, you are back in being mode.

Whenever you notice your mind wandering and you put your attention back to your body and breath, then you are setting up a neurological link between noticing mind-wandering and wanting to be in the moment. The more that you exercise and reuse this neurological link, so you train your mind to be in the moment. This is what we want.

Mind Wandering may well happen time and time again. As it does, each time just gently bring your focus back to your breathing and your body. Resist any temptation to get frustrated with yourself, as this will make matters worse and awaken your saboteur. Just notice any frustration building up and watch it fizzle out as you observe it passively. This requires an act of compassion towards yourself and your saboteur. It is through this type of kindness that you will befriend and win over your saboteur.

In noticing and treating mind wandering in these ways you can treat it as a benefit of the exercise rather than an obstacle to it.

Each time that you notice that your mind is not where you wanted it to be and has wandered, just use it as an opportunity to anchor paying attention to your breathing with being in the here and now.

Summary of Me-Time Exercise 1

1) Prepare by getting comfortable in a peaceful room.
2) Bring your attention to your body. Notice how it rests against any surfaces.
3) Create a spotlight of attention. Start with your toes and expand your spotlight to the whole of your body.
4) Observe any sensations in your body. Use passive observation - 2 mins.
5) Bring your attention to your breathing. Observe your in-breaths and out-breaths.
6) Observe your breathing. Notice any sensations as you breathe - 8 mins.

7) Notice any mind wandering. Treat yourself with compassion. Gently bring your focus of attention back to your breathing.

Do this exercise at least once a day for six consecutive days.

These exercises in mindfulness have been around for many years. The aim for us is to further your awareness of what is going on 'upstairs' and to give you some resources to enable you to get what you want out of life. If we had set out in this exercise to create complete stillness in the mind, then we would no doubt have failed dismally. Stillness, peace and silence is where it all starts but our minds are not designed to be completely still permanently, they are far too useful to us for that. By paying attention to our bodily sensations, by observing the breath we may have an end result of quietening the mind, and if this happened for you then that is fantastic, if not then that is fine too.

When I did this exercise for the first time I didn't really notice any quietening of my mind. Quite the reverse, I noticed just how much was going on in there! No sooner had I started to focus my attention on my feet when my mind flicked off at a tangent. I started thinking about how long the exercise still had to go. *Ten minutes! I could be doing all sorts of useful things in this time...I wonder if I am wasting my time?* This was my saboteur getting involved. It hates to be left out. Fear of wasting my time, fight or flight response again.

I then remembered that I should be focussing on my feet and I started doing that again. It certainly helped for me to think of the spotlight shining on the different parts of my body, and it gave me something to concentrate on. However, I noticed that I was visualising a big bright red spotlight with a flexible arm next to me rather than actually paying attention to the sensations! This was thinking interrupting me again, a bit of day dreaming. I began to get a bit frustrated. *How could I not go for even a few seconds without drifting off somewhere?*

In hindsight I know now that this very act of noticing that I was daydreaming was a breakthrough for me. This was me becoming aware of my thoughts, albeit only for a second.

As I continued the exercise, the thoughts of *"am I wasting my time here?"* recurred over and over in my mind. At one stage I remembered something that I had intended to do that afternoon and I started thinking about that. I am sure that I had been off with these thoughts for a couple of minutes before I remembered what I was doing and started paying attention to my breathing again.

With all the thinking interruptions and daydreaming I ended the exercise a bit disappointed with myself. The thing that I did not appreciate at the time was that there was no need for me to feel disappointed in any way. I had learned a lot and I had gained a huge amount of awareness. Awareness that I would use to improve as I continued to practise in the weeks to come.

I have to say that I found it really tricky to observe the sensations in my body. This was a big eye opener for me. I really was not in tune at all with my emotions, my body was like a great big void to me. I know now that this is quite normal. In our society and especially in business we are encouraged to ignore our emotions and use logical thinking. I had learned to blank out my emotions. This had proved useful to me in a business sense but from a personal point of view it left me feeling empty. I was determined to get back in tune with my body and emotions, but I would have to wait a little longer for that to develop.

As I paid attention to my body I could feel various itches. I knew that it felt a bit uncomfortable, as though I wanted to scratch the itch, but anything deeper than that was unavailable to me during this first exercise. I could also sense the surface that I was lying on but pinpointing exactly the feeling, and where on my body I was feeling it, was out of reach for me at this time.

The actual fact that I was paying attention to these things made me really curious. Yes, I was a bit frustrated, but it made me curious to learn more. This is what the exercise is designed to do. Merely paying attention to my thoughts and lack of sensations was opening up new neural networks, new possibilities and new potential opportunities for me, although I did not realise it at the time.

Abbie had a similar experience to me. She said "I just couldn't concentrate on the exercise. I couldn't seem to clear my thoughts. I remembered what you had suggested about seeing my mind as a lake. The lake was really choppy, I couldn't find any calm at all. My thoughts seemed to be stirring up the lake, one ripple after another. I found it really interesting to think of it in this way but shocking at the same time that I was so powerless to stop the thoughts."

The good news for Abbie is that this demonstrates that at least she had become aware of her thinking. Despite the fact that she knew that the aim of the exercise was not to get total stillness of mind, this had obviously been a hope of hers. She went on to say, "I have to say that I thought that I was completely wasting my time. A couple of minutes into the exercise I was thinking about all sorts of thing that were nothing to do with my body and breath, more to do with all the things that I felt that I should be doing instead!" As we know, this was her saboteur playing a part in her thinking. Her automatic pilot had kicked in.

Despite her disappointment, after the first exercise she went on to repeat the exercise every day for a week. "As I continued to practise I began to pay greater attention to my thought patterns. I became able to recognise when I had become distracted. As I recognised this I found that I was able to get some distance from these thoughts and observe them rather than get involved in them. This helped. I could then get back to concentrating on my breathing. I did keep getting distracted but I also began to have periods where my lake seemed much less disturbed. I could picture in my mind some stiller water in the distance."

Weather systems

Thinking of your mind as a lake can certainly help you gain perspective. The key is to observe the lake rather than try to control how the lake appears. As the weather system of thoughts in your mind changes, so do the conditions on the lake. As storm clouds pass by overhead, so the surface of your lake becomes disturbed. As the storm clouds are replaced by a lighter variety of cloud, so the lake settles down, you can notice smoother ripples on the surface and possibly even periods of stillness. Eventually you will get glimpses of sunlight.

Observe the different types of thought as different weather systems. You may even like to label them so that you can spot patterns in your thinking. As we know your unconscious mind will assist you in doing this. As you pay attention to your breathing and a weather system approaches, notice the type of thoughts that you are having, you can even say to yourself "here comes future planning", "here comes memories" or "here's worrying". Observe the thoughts as you would clouds overhead. Just pay attention to them as they pass by. You can watch them leave just as they have appeared and then you can go back to noticing to your breathing.

The thinking that goes on in the mind is completely random. It is random and it is repetitive. The unconscious mind is presenting us with thoughts based on what it thinks will serve us best. When it notices emotions in the body, it will give us thoughts associated with that to provide us with the opportunity to process whatever we need to process in order to release the emotions. When we fail to process the thoughts and release the emotions, the thoughts just keep on coming.

Our busy lives present plenty of opportunity for our saboteur to get up to mischief. It is like a misguided angel trying to look after our best interests and getting confused in the process. *Watch out for this consequence, watch out for that issue. This is a potential problem. Why are you not paying attention to it? What are you doing paying attention to your breathing? We have got worrying to do!*

By paying attention to our saboteur we can better give it instruction. By recognising our thoughts we are better able to process them. By shining a light on our emotions we can discover what things really mean to us and we can get perspective on our problems. By learning to appreciate the present moment through our body and our breathing we can realise that we are not our thoughts, our thoughts are mind creations and all mind creations have no real substance.

Habit Breaker 1 - Taking a different perspective

We really are creatures of habit. We love familiarity and this is not a problem, but it can feed our saboteur and it keeps us in our comfort zone. I want you to experience a break in routine, a challenge for your saboteur: it will help you to get to know your autopilots.

For the next week I want you to experiment by literally taking different perspectives. Do you always sit in the same chair to watch TV, or eat dinner? Experiment by sitting in a different chair. Do you always go to work or to the shops by taking the same route? Experiment by trying a different route or a different mode of transport.

Notice if you feel any discomfort from the suggestion. Did you notice any internal resistance to it? If you did then you can say hello to your saboteur.

As you take this different perspective, notice how it changes your experience. Do you feel any longing to go back to your old routine? Does it help you to stay more "present" in your thinking? Do you notice any sense of curiosity? What other feelings do you have?

We take things around us for granted. Our autopilots take over. As we follow habitual patterns of behaviour so we become less aware of what we can see, hear and feel at any one time. This habit breaker will give you a sense of getting back your awareness of your surroundings and appreciation for them.

Key Points

- Through our first "me-time" mindfulness exercise we set up an anchor to present moment awareness through noticing and paying attention to our breath. The exercise is designed to enable us to familiarise ourselves with being mindful of our body and breath, and how they are intrinsically linked. We may also notice just how frequently we are interrupted by our thoughts and how they distract us from concentrating on the task at hand. This enables you to distinguish further between doing and being mode.
- There are different ways of seeing thoughts in our mind: as clouds in the sky of our mind, as ripples on the surface of a lake. As we notice this we also notice that we can label our thoughts e.g: "planning" "worrying". This enables us to see the involvement of our saboteur and assess what our thoughts mean to us. It enables us to recognise and process our emotions.
- We begin a series of habit breaking exercises that assist us in becoming more aware of our autopilots and our doing mode. In this exercise we change some routines slightly in order to enable us to take a different perspective on them.

CHAPTER 17

Embracing Body and Mind

As we become more and more entrenched in our thoughts, so we lose the ability to connect with our body. Our days are so thoroughly consumed with thinking that we hardly give a thought to what is actually going on inside our physical form. Our problem solving minds are too busy identifying and bridging gaps in between what we want and what we have to notice the effects of our thinking and our behaviour on our bodies.

Of course the consequences of thinking on our bodies are huge as we think of the billions of neurological connections between mind and body. I had certainly neglected to consider the effects of my overworking on my health. Fortunately for me I was able to intervene before any serious effects could show themselves but I was getting increasingly agitated, intolerant of others, and frustrated with life. As I mentioned, I was so out of rapport with my body that I could not even identify my feelings, my bodily sensations when I did the Breath and Body exercise.

I needed to build this rapport back up again. I needed to rediscover my awareness for my own feelings and emotions and get to really know my body again. This second exercise helped me on my way to doing that.

"I was absolutely stressed to the limit." Steve is an accountant who went through our mindfulness programme recently. "People do not seem to realise the stress that accountants can suffer. My whole job involves thinking, details, planning. I became terrified of making a mistake. We act on behalf of other people and companies and I was scared to death of making a mistake with their figures that could end up costing them money. Every piece of work that I received made the situation worse. It was like a never-ending mountain of responsibility and fear."

With Steve the stress built up over many years. His checking and rechecking of figures was endless. He lived with the fear of getting something wrong. He was constantly living in a bubble of fear. He feared the consequences of making mistakes, so his saboteur was effectively living on his shoulders. He would pick up the phone and fear a customer complaining to him. He would worry that he had missed something in the figures. He would get anxious about the work that he had to do and the work that he had completed.

Is my knowledge up to date? Do I really know what I am doing? Did I get that bit of work wrong? Have I interpreted the figures correctly? What happens if I can't complete this piece of work in time? Constant worry and anxiety.

"The thing with my job is that as you get better at it and more experienced, so you get bigger and bigger clients, with more money at stake." Steve feared taking time off as this would mean that his pile of work just got bigger and bigger. "I had not had a holiday for five years and it began to take a toll on me."

Steve's health had deteriorated and he was forced to take time off. Not only were the effects internal, they were also visible externally as well. He had a constant stoop. His shoulders were rounded and hunched, just as they would have been as he was pouring over the papers on his desk. The saboteur sitting on his shoulders was weighing him down. He was pale as a sheet, I noticed that his breathing was really shallow, his skin was suffering from a lack of oxygen. He had not had time for exercise.

As Steve had been living in his thoughts, so he had been bottling up his fear for years. His saboteur was absolutely stirred up to a frenzy, he was living on his nerves.

These are the kinds of sacrifice that we make when work becomes our overriding number one concern in our lives. These are the consequences of believing that our thoughts and fears are real. These are the results of ignoring our negative emotions: our body begins to show signs of stress.

Somehow we kid ourselves into believing that it is ok to treat our bodies as separate, it is ok to mistreat our bodies. Everything catches up with us eventually.

We must first of all learn to pay attention to our bodies, to the sensations and feelings that give us signs of its discomfort. We can then learn to read the messages that it is sending us, so that we can take appropriate action. Appropriate action in terms of nourishing the body through what we put in it rather than depleting it. Appropriate action in terms of exercise. Appropriate action in terms of managing our thoughts, processing our emotions to release any negative emotions that we may have been storing up.

Moment to moment judgements and decisions that we make are unconsciously guided by our mind filters. They can have a profound effect on our body. As we discover more and more about our mind filters, about how we make our judgements, so we can regain influence over them and improve our all round health and well-being. Getting to know our body and understanding these links is a key part of this process.

For my part, I needed to recognise my need to relax and take stock. I needed some way to reconnect with my body and begin growing my awareness of how my thoughts and actions impacted on my whole being. I have always done some kind of sport and always exercised. I think that this assisted me in some way, it provided a reward system for my body and after exercise I always felt more relaxed but it didn't really allow me the space to take a more intimate inspection. This particular mindfulness exercise provided me with the means to start doing this.

Body Scan - Me-Time Exercise 2 (15 Minutes)

During this exercise we are going to use similar tactics to those in the previous Breath and Body exercise. You will need to create the time every day for six days to carry out this practice. You will also need to find a quiet space for the exercise where you can rest for 15 minutes or so without being disturbed. These exercises are an investment by time in yourself. If you build them into a regular practice they will reward you many times over throughout your future.

Any time in the future when you are present in your mind, and when in the past you would have been running and rerunning habitual thought patterns, you are effectively receiving payback from your investment.

As you do this exercise you will continue to notice any thoughts that take your mind away from the moment at hand. Just observe them and watch as they pass by. This exercise, as the title indicates, involves using your spotlight of attention to investigate the sensations in the various parts of your body in detail, allowing you to perform a full scan of your body.

Preparation

1) This exercise is best carried out lying down. Either lie down on your bed, or on a rug on the floor. Make sure that you will be warm enough to lie comfortably. You can place a cover over you for warmth if you like. Whilst most people prefer to do this exercise with their eyes closed, you may open them if you feel as though you are falling asleep.

Beginning to relax - notice your breathing

2) Start by connecting with your breathing. Pay attention to your in-breath and out-breath as you begin to relax. As you continue to breathe - naturally, without forcing the breath in any way, notice which parts of your body are connected to the surface that you are lying on. With every out-breath just relax a little further and notice how you seem to sink deeper into the surface.

3) This exercise is about becoming aware of sensations in your body. We will use your awareness and natural curiosity to connect you to these sensations. Awareness is about connecting with yourself and the world as it exists, so just let yourself be. If you find yourself judging, trying to alter anything or getting the desire to gain control over your thoughts or your body, then resist the temptation. Just observe things as they exist in the moment. This is a time for being alert to your senses and to your body, awake to any feelings that you get inside. Just observe how your mind can let everything else go now.

4) Your attention is on your breathing, in and out. Focus in on how your breathing is influencing any sensations in your abdomen. Notice how the walls of your abdomen expand and contract as your breath continues to go in and out all of its own accord. Just spend a few moments exploring the sensations you get as your abdomen rises and falls with your breath.

Begin the scan

5) As your spotlight of attention rests gently on your abdomen, just gradually move it down your body. Move it down your legs, past your knees. Further down to your ankles, feet and down to your toes. As your spotlight shines gently on your toes explore any sensations there. Can you feel your toes touching? Can you feel the air around your toes? Are your

toes touching any fabric? Go deeper into your awareness, notice the qualities in the sensations. Is there any tingling in your toes? Are they warm or cool? Is any tingling constant or intermittent? Are they numb? Is there any vibration that you feel there? Resist the temptation to judge or to imagine your sensations, just observe them as they are. If you notice nothing, then that is fine, just let it be as it is.

6) Get playful now. As you breathe in and out just notice where the breath goes. On an in-breath notice how the breath goes deep down into your body, filling your lungs. Does it stop there? Notice how as you breathe in you can imagine the air filling your body bit by bit, going through your lungs, filling your stomach, your legs and going right down to your toes. As you breathe out, you can imagine the air leaving your toes, going up your legs, through your stomach, lungs, up and out of your body.

7) Staying curious and playful, on your next out-breath guide your spotlight to the soles of your feet, encompassing your heels and the instep of your feet. Let your awareness shine gently on the bottom of your feet as you pay attention to any sensations there. Notice if you can feel them touching anything, how does it feel? Hard or soft? Warm or cool? What other sensations are there? If you feel any sensations then breathe into them. Whatever you notice, when you breathe in let the breath flow right through the sensations. Notice what happens to them. Your focus now is on the soles of your feet and your breathing.

8) When you are ready and on another out-breath let your attention float up from the soles of your feet to the top of your feet, right up to your ankles. As you focus on your feet notice that you can let your attention go deeper, moving from the surface of your feet, through the flesh, deep into your bones. Notice any sensations from deep inside both feet now.

9) On another out-breath slide your spotlight up from your feet, through your ankles and onto your lower legs. Let go of your feet as your attention shifts to your legs. Hold your attention here for about twenty to thirty seconds, paying close attention to any and all sensations in your lower legs, with your background awareness still on your breathing.

10) Move up your body, bit by bit, gently and slowly guiding the light of your attention as you go. Spend time curiously investigating each part of your body in turn. Scan your knees, slowly moving up to your thighs. Spend the same twenty to thirty seconds on each area. Move up to your pelvic area, your buttocks and hips. Let the spotlight move on only after you have closely examined each area. Move your attention on, floating up to your lower back, stomach, then chest, and then shoulders. Move on using an out-breath and float down to your hands, right down to the very tips of your fingers and scan them. What do you feel? Breathing in and out, feel your breath take your attention right down to the ends of your fingers. Then let your attention gradually move through your fingers to your hands, wrists, forearms,, elbows and upper arms. Continue breathing and focussing your attention in each area as you go, up now to your armpits and shoulders, neck and head. As you scan your head take each area one by one, your jaw, mouth, lips, nose, cheeks, ears, eyes and forehead. What is there to discover here? Hold your head in the full light of your awareness.

Breathe into your sensations and feelings

11) As you perform the scan and whenever you notice a sensation, get really curious. What is it? Is it tension? Is it vibration? Is it emotion? Is it nothing at all? Take the sensation and breathe into it. As you breathe out of the sensation notice what happens to it if anything. Does it take it away? Does it change it at all?

Mind Wandering

12) When you catch yourself falling into day dreaming or mind wandering, then just notice it. Make a mental note of it and acknowledge it for what it is. Let it go and return your awareness to the part of the body that you left some moments ago.

Concluding

13) After you have scanned each area of your body just let your spotlight diffuse a little and expand to encompass the whole of your body. Hold the whole of your body in your awareness and let any sensations just melt into each other as you embrace your wholeness inside, breathing in and out.

Did you fall asleep? If you did, then don't worry, I hope that you enjoyed your nap! This is a really relaxing exercise and it is easy to become drowsy and slip into a light sleep. If you keep dropping off, then you could do the exercise with your eyes lowered and open or your head propped up by a cushion or pillow.

Summary of the Body Scan - Me-Time Exercise 2

1) Do this exercise lying down with your eyes closed. Get comfortable. Stay alert.
2) Pay attention to your breathing. Just observe it without forcing it in any way.
3) Notice the movement and any sensations in your abdomen as you breathe.
4) Move your spotlight of attention gently down to the tips of your toes.
5) Get playful. Observe the breath filling your body, right down to the ends of your toes.
6) Move your attention gently on to the soles of your feet.

7) Gradually moving up the body, spend 20 to 30 seconds observing each part of your body. Keep your breathing in the background of your attention throughout.
8) What sensations can you observe in each place as your spotlight of attention rests there?
9) Breathe into any sensation as it comes to you. Notice how it changes, if at all.
10) Deal with mind wandering by just noticing it. Make a mental note of it. Let it go.
11) Hold your whole body in your awareness.

Hopefully you did not fall into the trap of expecting a complete fifteen minutes of peace and serenity inside as you did this exercise for the first time. Realistically, you are going to need plenty of practice until your unconscious mind learns fully what your me-time is really intended for. It needs you to really train it the way that you want it.

Having said that I hope that you were able to feel some relaxation in your body and mind as a result of investing your time in doing the body scan. Just the fact that you lay down and rested for a few minutes will have given your mind a stress break, so that will have done you good.

Were you able to notice some of the traits of the doing mode in your mind as you completed this exercise? Whenever your mind took you to some place other than your body and breath, that was doing mode. Were you able to identify any planning? Any worrying? Any thoughts of what you have been doing over the last few days? If you did, then you spotted your mind in doing mode.

Any time that you were paying attention to your breathing and to your body without background chatter and other background thoughts, you were in being mode. I hope that you will have experienced this mode, if only for a short while. How did it feel for you?

When I noticed being mode for the first time since I became aware of the difference between doing mode and being mode, it was like a light being turned on in my head. In fact it was like a light being turned on in my life. All of a sudden the world seemed a brighter place. It was like turning up the volume on my senses. It was like coming home somehow.

It was only a glimpse for me, but it was such a relief to see it. What I am really talking about is, seeing "the now". It was as though someone flicked a switch and turned off my thinking brain for a second. My head felt empty. It was as though I was looking through an empty head straight out into the world. Straight out into "the now". I felt energy, I felt excitement, I felt enthusiasm and I saw what peace looks like. I wanted more.

I was noticing my breathing, observing my breath going in and out. I put my hand on my stomach and felt it moving with my breath. As I did this I realised that although I had been doing the exercise, I had also been judging it.

This is interesting. 15 minutes. Hmmm. That's a long time to be doing nothing. I wonder if I will feel anything. Oh yes, my breathing is what I should be paying attention to. There it is. It isn't very deep. Let me see if my stomach moves.

And then it happened. I realised that I had been judging and thinking. It just stopped as I opened up my awareness to my breathing and rested my hand on my stomach.

What happened next was, well, nothing. Nothing was happening. It felt amazing. I was paying full attention to my breathing and I moved my attention to the tips of my toes. All of my attention went down there. It was as though I was right down there in my toes, paying attention to the feeling of them resting together, feeling nice and warm, tingling a little bit.

That was it. My mind then went into overdrive.

Waaah! What was that? Was that being mode? That was nice. Let's see if I can get it back. What did I do again? I'm sure that I am doing it right. It has gone. Hmm. I wonder how long I have been doing this for now. Ooops, I forgot what I was doing. Where was I? Oh yes, back to the toes, and breathing. Let's see what happens next. Noooo. I'm thinking again. Why can't it stop?

And so it went on. My judging and habitual thinking took over again. It didn't take over 100% of my attention but sufficient to keep me in doing mode for the remainder of the exercise.

With practice you will definitely get to know being mode. Whenever you notice it, then congratulate yourself because this is a step in the right direction for you. Whenever you notice it you send a message to your unconscious mind, "I want more of this. Please pay attention to it."

This is the habit that we want your unconscious mind to pick up. One day I want you to catch yourself peacefully getting on with enjoying your life in the present moment, living with full vitality, taking in everything around you.

Now, a message to your saboteur:

There is no need to panic! Whenever we need to think and plan then we will still be able to do that. We will set time aside to get on with our doing mode activities, we will take time to review our day and to plan for tomorrow. We will continue to listen to your concerns, objectively, and we will treat them with the respect that they deserve. However, relax my little friend, this moment is for living. Enjoy it now.

Practice and more practice

Once is not enough. You need to keep practicing this exercise. You will continue to learn and develop. I promise you. Do it every day for the next six days before you move on to the next exercise.

Notice how you are improving your awareness with practice. However, do not get despondent if you go back a step and find doing mode taking over the whole exercise. Every day is different. Some days you will have a clearer mind than others. It usually depends on how frantic the day has been as to how long it takes your mind to slow down and how successfully you gather your awareness, but it can also depend on a multitude of things, including the people that you have been around.

Remember, that we have lots of demands on the limited number of bits of information that we can process at any one time. Some days we might quite literally have a queue of thoughts that are waiting to be processed before we can get any peace inside. Inevitably when you sit down to do this exercise, your unconscious mind might well think, "Great, we are relaxing, there is some space up there. Here you go, consider this...." And your head will be full of thoughts all of a sudden.

If at all possible I recommend that you do these exercises first thing in the morning and last thing in the evening. Your mind will be quieter first thing in the morning. Sleep helps us to process the information of the day. When you sleep, your unconscious mind gets to work putting everything in place, filing information, storing it and indexing it. Notice the difference between your experiences of the exercise at different times of day.

Habit Breaker 2 - Having a walk

One way of really bringing the here and now into your life is to go for a walk. Take some time over the next few days to go for a walk with the intention of doing no more that appreciating the fresh air and the scenery. Make sure that you leave sufficient time so that you can complete the walk without having to be concerned with the time that it is taking.

I often use walking and jogging time to plan and review as I find that it gives me a different perspective. It works really well in that respect but every so often I deliberately decide that rather than using the walk for thinking, I will use the walk to be present and to appreciate the world around me. This is about choosing being mode over doing mode.

As you know by now, you can expect doing mode to play a part in our walk. As you walk the key is to pay attention to any thoughts that creep into your consciousness. Watch them as you have been doing in the me-time exercises and let them dissolve as you pay full attention to the outside world.

If you have been practicing the Expanded Awareness exercise then, as you walk, you can just expand your awareness in the same way to encompass all of the sights and sounds around you, feeling the fresh air against your face and skin. Notice that you can look around in various directions and maintain this state of expanded awareness.

Whatever you are doing as you walk, the intention is to pay attention only to things occurring in the present moment. Pay attention to the outside world. What can you see? What can you hear? Can you feel the ground beneath your feet? Is there any wind? What temperature is the air around you?

Pay attention to how the walk is affecting your breathing. Are you breathing more deeply? What feelings and sensations are you experiencing inside?

As well as looking around and down, don't forget to look up as you walk, what can you see in the sky? Are there any birds flying overhead?

Watch out for your saboteur reminding you of the things that you must do when you get back from your walk. If this happens, then thank your saboteur for the reminder and gently direct your attention back to the present moment, your walk and the sensory delights on offer to you.

A good walk can have a really transformative effect on your mood. We really do miss out on so many of the free delights of life as we get trapped in our doing mode of thinking. By paying attention only to the present moment through our senses we begin to learn that we can appreciate the beauty of nature, it is ever present around us. We can find pleasure and joy in the smallest of things when we step away from our judgement for a moment or two.

Key Points

- As we live such busy lives it is easy to start neglecting our health. If we fail to look after our bodies then we will begin to experience the negative effects of neglect. We will start to show the strain of overthinking and overwork. We can end up falling out of rapport with our body.
- The Body Scan exercise is designed to re-familiarise us with the inner workings of body so that we can rebuild our rapport with it.
- The body scan exercise focusses on becoming aware of sensations in the body, breathing and using the breath to explore the body. If we notice thoughts creeping in then we can just watch them as they pass by and then go back to focussing on breathing and our body.

CHAPTER 18

The carrot and the stick trap

You are probably aware of the carrot and stick idiom where a cart driver dangles a carrot in front of a mule whilst holding a stick behind it. It is a way of inducing behaviour. The donkey moves towards the carrot and away from the stick thus moving the cart forward.

There are positives and negatives in each approach and it is the combination of the two approaches that produces the forward momentum. If you only offer positive incentives, then it can end up having only a short term impact, since people tend to start taking them for granted and they end up losing motivation. If you only use negative incentives or the threat of punishment, then people will end up rebelling against it.

Much of the way that we approach life through our thinking reflects these two approaches and if we are not careful then we end up getting trapped in a carrot and stick cycle.

We create carrots for ourselves in our mind by imagining rewards for our progress, in terms of imagining how we might feel once we have achieved something, or what it might enable us to buy.

We create a stick for ourselves by developing expectations over our performance, our level of self perfectionism and what we might lose if we were to fail in our work or not take action at all.

The carrot and stick approach can be a great motivator and it can start dominating our thoughts and our actions. What we are talking about here of course is future thinking. We are using thoughts of possible future rewards and future penalties to move us in a certain direction in life. This kind of thinking can become repetitive and addictive. It creates a trap for our thoughts and our life.

As we are contemplating our stick, things that we could lose, things that may go wrong, then bear in mind that we are all the while stimulating our saboteur. Our fight or flight response is provoked as soon as we create internal representations of loss or failure. This in turn creates fear in our system. We begin to feel uncomfortable as our saboteur lets us know that we had better do something to avoid the possible consequences. We feel motivated to act but we do not feel happy about having to do it.

If we are motivated due to the stick then we can expect to look for shortcuts, after all we are not really enjoying the feeling of being compelled to take action. We may come to resent what we are having to do, we may start wishing life were different, we may start craving relaxation. Think about what impact all of these thoughts are having on the body. We are bound to start feeling zapped of energy sooner rather than later.

This is a downward spiral. As we feel low on energy, as we wish that life were different, as we take our eye off the ball, so this creates further fear in our system. Our saboteur is fully active now, monopolising our thoughts, making us feel really unhappy.

Think about the carrot effect also. As we move towards getting the things that we want in life, as we achieve our goals, so we set new goals and objectives in order to renew our motivation and enthusiasm. Achieving, accumulating, improving, growing becomes addictive. We move from one objective to the next. How much time do we actually spend appreciating what we have? In fact, what happens if we do actually stop for a minute and begin appreciating life? Our saboteur comes out and says, *what are you doing? You are wasting time. You should be working!*

Once we have accumulated wealth and possessions it is only a question of time before we start to fear losing them. The stick and our saboteur again playing a part in our thinking. In this way we end up being trapped in a vicious cycle of carrot and stick motivation and thinking.

There are very few things more uncomfortable for us than the feeling of being trapped. When we are feeling trapped our natural inclination is to try to escape. How do we try to escape the carrot and stick? We do more thinking, we set more goals, we work harder. This just makes the situation worse.

Until we are able to create breaks in the cycles of thinking, worrying and planning we are creating stress in our system. It is not the creation of stress that becomes the problem, it is failing to recover from it. The exercises that we bring you in this book are designed to provide you with a trapdoor for you to use to escape your past and future thinking, to give you a break from doing mode of thinking and allow you to just enjoy being for a while.

As you practise the exercises and experience the benefits of being mindful, so you may choose to spend more and more of your time being present, expanding your awareness and observing the way that your body speaks to you.

The me-time exercises in this book will really enhance your ability to relax, will provide you with lots of insights into your saboteur, into your thinking and of course they require some quiet space and time for you to carry them out.

I am sure that as you continue to practise the exercises you will start feeling and seeing the benefits in your life. There will also be times when you still feel frazzled, still feel a bit low and in need of a quick fix. In addition to the Expanded Awareness exercise I want to provide you with another tool that you can use as your trapdoor to the now and to enter being mode as you go about your day.

The Three Minute Breathing Space exercise

We can get so wound up with our thoughts and engrossed in our problems that sometimes we forget the benefits of just sitting back for a minute and taking stock. All of these mindfulness exercises are designed to give us a breather from our routines, give our mind and body a rest and allow us to re-energise. Hopefully you are starting to see some of the benefits of this.

When a low mood takes hold, when anger strikes, when we are rushing from task to task we can find it really tricky to remember the benefits of the mindfulness that we are learning. Ironically it is at times like this that our new skills are most useful. It is only by regularly using the skills and building them into a habit that we will be able to call upon them automatically when we need them most.

In order to assist you in building the habit of mindfulness, I recommend doing this exercise twice a day, every day. It only takes three minutes, and you can do it sitting in your car, sitting at your desk, or sitting in your living room at home. It gives you a bit of breathing space between your thinking and it uses all of the techniques of mindfulness that we have learned so far.

Step 1 - Awareness on your inner thoughts, feelings and sensations

Adopt an upright and relaxed posture, either sitting or standing. The upright posture encourages you to stay alert, and stimulates your awareness. If possible, close your eyes.

In this exercise you will focus on your inner experience, so bring your awareness inside, recognise and acknowledge what is going on inside. Ask yourself: what is my experience right now?

Thoughts: What thoughts are you having? Pay attention to your thoughts, see them just as events, clouds moving through the mind.

Feelings: What feelings are you having inside? Are you feeling any discomfort or unpleasant feelings? Just pay attention to them, acknowledge them without feeling the need to change anything particularly.

Sensations: What sensations can you notice in your body? Do a quick body scan. Is there any tightness? Any tension? Any churning? Just play the observer, paying attention to your sensations without getting involved in altering anything.

Step 2 - Focusing attention on your breath

Now it is time to re-establish your breathing anchor. Pay attention to your breathing. When you breathe in, notice the air going into your body, down your throat, deep inside your lungs. Watch how your stomach and chest expand as your body is filled with air and how they contract as you let the air leave your body all of its own accord. Let this experience ground you in the here and now. If you find any thoughts creeping in, then just observe them and let them go with the next out-breath as you move through your trapdoor into the present moment.

Step 3 - Expanding your attention to the body

As you continue to observe your breathing, let your attention expand to your whole body. Imagine the breath filling your entire body. Notice any sensations of tension or discomfort that exist in your body and let the air gently move around those sensations, eventually surrounding them and penetrating them if it wants to. Breathing out, notice the air leaving your body, leaving the sensations, notice what effect this has on the sensations. In this way we are learning to befriend our sensations: get to know our body and through our body get to know and befriend our saboteur. When your sensations stop pulling at your attention, then just return your awareness to your body as a whole.

Summary of the Three Minute Breathing Space exercise

1) Bring your attention inside. Focus on your thoughts, feelings and sensations. Notice what is happening. Resist the temptation to change anything - 1 min
2) Focus on your breath. Watch your breath filling and leaving your body. Notice that you become present - 1 min
3) Expand your attention to the whole of your body and your breathing. Let the breath surround and fill any sensations that you feel - 1 min

Think of this exercise in terms of three stages: Opening the trapdoor, approaching it, moving through it to the other side.

Stage one is just noticing what is happening inside at the present moment, you can see this as the opening of your trapdoor to the present moment. It is like a reality check on your thoughts, feelings and sensations.

In stage two we approach the trapdoor, we can see the other side of the door here. We use our breath to guide us to the entrance to the door. We get a sense of passing through the door to the other side.

Stage three sees us come out of the other side of the trapdoor. We are present now, in being mode. We have our attention on our breathing and the sensations in our body. We are able to observe sensations, befriend them with our breath. We are just observing breath and body, resisting any feelings of a need to change anything.

Mindfulness in Movement - Me-Time Exercise 3 (16 Minutes)

There are two components to this third Me-Time exercise: the first is the Mindful Movement exercise explained below, the second is the body and breath exercise (Me-Time exercise 1). Each component should last about 8 minutes.

We are first of all going to bring your body to life through some very light exercises. This should ease any tension and will enable you to get to know your body further, assisting you in befriending it. We then move into the breath and body exercise that you are already familiar with. As we are preceding this part with the movement exercise it will bring another dimension to your practice.

The movement exercise is essentially a light stretching exercise. Stretching has the benefit of realigning your muscles, and allowing the release of any tension that may have been building up in your body.

Stretching in itself is an act of placing temporary stress on your body. As it is temporary it serves to waken up your cells and strengthen them. When you come away from the stretch it releases the stress in the cells, allowing them to recover.

I would like to emphasize at this point that the aim of this exercise is not to put you in pain. You should only go as far into each stretch as is ok for you to do. Listen to and be kind to your body. If you start to feel any pain then back off a little from your stretch or come back to your standing position. If you have any physical injuries, any back pain for example, then please seek advice from your doctor before doing the exercise.

As you do the exercise then the idea is to bring about more awareness to the sensations and feelings in your body. When you feel discomfort, then bring awareness to that feeling, notice if the feelings come and go along with the sensations in your body. As always the spirit in which you do the exercise is more important than getting exact positions or the perfect stretch or a serene flowing pattern of movement. You will improve your practice over time.

Here is the exercise:

Preparation

You will be standing for this exercise, reaching up and outwards, so you will need a quiet space in which it is suitable to do that.

You can do this in socks or bare feet. Stand with your feet about hips width apart, feet parallel to each other. You want to have your legs slightly bent at the knees so that they are not locked in position. Have your arms hanging loosely by your sides. Start noticing your breathing.

Raising your arms

On an in-breath gently raise your arms out to your sides so that they are parallel to the floor. On your next in-breath continue to raise your arms slowly and smoothly so that they are above your head, hands facing each other. As you raise your arms mindfully, pay attention to the stretch in the muscles and any sensations that this brings to them. Notice any sensations as you hold your arms above your head.

Continue breathing in and out, all the while continuing to

stretch your arms and hands upwards. Stretch your fingers gently towards the sky, leaving your feet firmly planted on the floor. Look up towards your fingertips. Feel the stretch in all of your muscles and joints up from your feet, through your legs, hips, stomach, chest, shoulders and arms. What sensations are there?

Maintain this stretch for five breaths. Notice your breathing and the sensations in your body, as your breath goes in and out all of its own accord. Pay attention to any changes in sensations, and observe any growing feelings of relaxation, discomfort, tension.

After your five breaths and on an out-breath just start gradually, smoothly and slowly lowering your arms back to your sides. Lower your gaze. As you move your arms notice the change in sensations as your muscles relax so that your arms are hanging loosely again from your shoulders. Close your eyes and let the after effects of your stretch sink in. As you do this continue to notice your breathing.

After a few moments of rest and again on an in-breath, open your eyes and raise your arms once again to parallel with the floor. Repeat the first stretch.

Continue for several stretches.

Picking apples

If your eyes are closed, then open them. Take your left hand and on an in-breath slowly raise it to the sky. Reach out with it as if you are stretching to pick an apple from just out of reach in a tree. Be fully aware of the sensations in the movement, in your muscles, of your breathing. Follow your hand with your gaze. As you gently stretch your hand into the air, raise your right heel off the floor so that you can reach just a little further up. Feel the stretch right up from your right foot, through your body and up through your left hand and fingers.

Come out of this stretch after five breaths. On an out-breath, first of all lower your right heel to the floor and then lower your hand. Let your eyes follow your hand gently down, then close them as you drink in the after-effects of your stretch. Again notice any sensations you feel in your body now.

Repeat this stretch with your right arm. On an in-breath, raise the right arm and then left heel off the floor. Feel the stretch, notice the sensations and continue to pay attention to your breathing.

Bending Sideways

From your standing position imagine that you are standing between two pieces of transparent plastic or glass. Place your hands on your hips. On an in-breath bend over towards your left. As you bend you can move your hips slightly to the right. The bend should be sideways, rather than bending forwards or backwards. You should form a gentle curve from your feet through to your head.

As you bend, concentrate on your breath and your movement. It is not important how far you bend. Feel the stretch in your legs, and your side. Remain in this position for five breaths.

On an out-breath return to standing upright. Close your eyes and feel the after-effects of your stretch, notice any sensations that exist.

Repeat this by bending slowly and gently to your right.

Rolling your shoulders

Gather your breath again. We are going to experiment with rolling your shoulders. Keeping your arms dangling by your side, on an in-breath roll your shoulders backwards and upwards. As you breathe out complete the move by rolling your shoulders forwards and downwards.

Breathe in and reverse the roll. Roll your shoulders forwards and upwards. Breathe out rolling your shoulders backwards and downwards.

Breathe in and squeeze your shoulders together and forwards as if you are try to get them to touch. Breathe out and move your shoulders apart and back to normal.

Breathe in and squeeze your shoulders together and backwards. Breathe out and return them to normal.

Keep experimenting with rolling your shoulders. Half a roll on an in-breath, complete the roll on an out-breath.

Relax

Spend a few moments drinking in the after-effects of your stretches. Get fully in tune with your body and notice any sensations that are there now.

Proceed to do the body and breath exercise (Me-Time exercise 1).

Summary of Mindfulness in Movement - Me-Time Exercise 3 (16 Minutes)

1) Stand with feet parallel to each other, hips width apart, arms dangling to your side.
2) **Raising your arms** - Gather your breath and raise your arms to your sides with an in-breath. Raise them to the sky with your next in-breath. Look up and feel the stretch through to your fingertips.
3) Remain here for five breaths. Lower your arms on an out-breath. Feel the sensations as you move.
4) Repeat - 2 mins.

5) **Picking apples** - Raise your left hand to the sky on an in-breath. Raise your right heel from the floor. Hold the stretch for five breaths.
6) Come down on an out-breath. Repeat with the right hand.
7) Repeat - 2 mins.
8) **Bending sideways** - Place your hands on your hips. Bend to your left on an in-breath. What sensations do you feel? Hold the position for five breaths.
9) Come back up on an out-breath. Repeat by bending to your right.
10) Repeat - 2 mins.
11) **Rolling your shoulders** - Experiment with rolling your shoulders. Keep your arms dangling loosely and roll your shoulders backwards and up, forwards and down. Use an in-breath to complete the first half of the roll, an out-breath for the second half.
12) Feel the sensations in your muscles and body as you continue to experiment with rolling your shoulders, forwards, backwards, together. - 2 mins.
13) Relax. Drink in the after-effects.
14) Complete the breath and body exercise - 8 mins.

How did you find that exercise? Did you find it easier to stay mindful as you were moving? As I explored the various mindfulness techniques I found that with this exercise I was more able to stay in the present moment. I had fewer interruptions from my saboteur and from repetitive doing mode thinking. Students on our mindfulness programmes report the same. It is likely to be down to the fact that the mind is preoccupied. Our moving, being aware of our breathing, consumes much of our capacity for processing chunks of information, so there is less risk of getting distracted.

Many people also say that following the stretching, they are also more able to stay in the moment during the body and breath part of the exercise. Somehow the stretching relaxes and befriends the body and the mind. This can be no bad thing.

How did you find the stretching part of the exercise? Did you notice any tension? What sensations did you experience? It can be quite shocking to realise how inflexible we become over the years if we do not exercise regularly. Our ability to stretch is another thing that improves with practice. Do not be afraid to feel the stretch. Don't forget that your saboteur will tell you to back off before your limits. It is only by reaching our limits that we expand them. Pay attention of course to your own safety and back off if you start to feel pain.

Did you notice any knots in your muscles? I find that my neck and shoulders are particularly susceptible to knotting. All the tension and stress in my body tends to build up in my neck and shoulders. Typing on the computer does not help, and I can often feel it most in the shoulder roll. Breathing deeply whilst rolling my shoulders and stretching really helps to relieve me of my knots. I get a wonderfully refreshing sense of release after the exercise now.

Stretching is all about exploring and challenging your limits rather than judging them. Notice when you feel discomfort, notice the sensations that you get. Your saboteur will encourage you to judge. Observe the messages that you are getting, explore them and gently challenge them. Go to your limits but do not try to go beyond them and be aware of which limits are imposed by your saboteur. Breathe into the sensations, let your breath do the exploring for you; this embraces your discomfort, offering it goodwill and compassion This is how you will befriend your inner saboteur. Many people find that any initial discomfort melts away and is eventually replaced with soothing, mellow sensations.

Habit Breaker 3 - Having a picnic

We have already experimented with sitting in different chairs, now I suggest eating a meal with no chairs at all, sitting on the floor. You can do this outside or inside, it doesn't matter, but I want you to have a picnic. You can go the whole way and fill a picnic hamper, get a soft blanket and go for a walk in the countryside, or just pick a comfortable place to sit on the floor at home: the spirit of the exercise again is more important than the detail.

I suggest getting some sandwiches and some bits to nibble, something that you can eat with your hands rather than a knife and fork, but you can choose anything to eat at all. You can do this alone, or with company.

As you are sitting down to eat, be mindful of your experience. You can use your breath to ground you in the moment. Savour your food as you are eating it, notice how it smells as you bring it to your mouth, chew it slowly and deliberately. Take the time to observe your surroundings. If you are sitting at home, notice how the room looks different from where you are sitting on the floor. Notice how all of this changes your eating experience.

This exercise brings to our awareness many of the autopilots that we have around eating. It shows how varying our patterns of behaviour from time to time can re-awaken our sense of curiosity and excitement for some of the simple pleasures in life.

Key Points

- We motivate ourselves by thinking of rewards that we may get in the future if we take certain actions. We can also motivate ourselves by thinking of the negative impact of neglecting to take action.
- This is motivation by carrot and stick, it is future thinking and it can become addictive. If we rely on negatives to drive us forward, then we may end up resenting what we are doing. It can take away our energy, it can provoke our saboteur and it can make us unhappy. If we get trapped in a cycle of carrot and stick motivation and future thinking, then it can cause stress, worry and overthinking. These mindfulness exercises help break these cycles and get us out of the trap.

- The Three Minute Breathing Space exercise - Re-enforces the anchor of being in the present moment by noticing our breathing, enables us to become grounded and aware.
- The Mindfulness in Movement exercise takes us to the second phase of building up our rapport with our body. It involves some very light stretching movements. As we move gently through the poses we remain in the present moment, our focus is on our breathing, our flowing, gentle movement and the response of our body.

CHAPTER 19

False beliefs and awareness of your saboteur

Through the mindfulness exercises in this book so far we have been exploring our thinking, bringing it into our awareness, identifying our doing and being modes and our autopilots. You may have been able to identify the three time frames involved with your thoughts: past, present and future.

We have been setting the emphasis on being in the present during our exercises, re-familiarising ourselves with our pure experience, re-acquainting ourselves with our body. Whilst maintaining an awareness of the present moment in the exercises is desirable, and indeed having presence of mind generally is desirable, it is unlikely that we will easily be able to clear our thinking and remain totally in the present for sustained periods of time without a great deal of practice. This is perfectly ok. We will gradually build this skill.

The aim of our mindfulness is not to create a perfect stillness of mind, it is to improve our awareness of how we are thinking, to become mindful of how we are thinking so that we can get our life the way that we want it.

One way that we are going to be able to influence our results and create a greater level of happiness is to recognise the rules that we are holding for ourselves in our heads. We have already set about examining and changing our values for life in order to get ourselves pointing in the direction that we want to go. This is a really good start and by bringing our unconscious values into consciousness we have been able to provide instruction to our unconscious mind as to the way that we would like things to be for us.

As we know, the thing is that whilst the unconscious mind will attempt to follow our conscious instruction it is also conditioned to provide us with protection. As we go about our day our unconscious mind will weigh up thoughts, events and experiences and it will judge whether or not any of them are likely to cause us harm. It will assess the possibility for emotional or psychological pain. This is where we experience the involvement of our inner saboteur.

Let me give you an example. I have set **progress** as my number one value in life. This means that when I wake up every day progress is important to me. So if I spend my day working on things that provide me with progress, then I am likely to feel happy. **Love** is my number two value, so if I feel loved and am able to demonstrate love to others as I am making progress going about my day, then I am going to be really happy.

Things do not always go to plan for us. What happens if I judge that my activities during the day have not yielded any progress? What happens if I have a row with a loved one? I am likely to start feeling unhappy as I will judge that my top values are not being met. If this happens as a one off, then it might not be too serious as I can wake up the next day and make progress and feel love. If this starts happening frequently, then it might start causing problems for me.

After several days of working hard and making no progress my saboteur is going to be on high alert. My saboteur is going to be operating in defense mode. It can see the potential for pain for me in my value of progress:

What happens if he wants progress and can't get it? There is a potential for pain here. Sadness, frustration. Send him some messages of comfort. Get him to make progress less important for himself, this will make sure that he feels ok.

As a result my saboteur may send me messages via my thoughts. I may start thinking things like, *"I am not sure that I can make progress doing this work." "Possibly I am not good enough to make progress." "Maybe I should lower my expectations."* These thoughts come to me in the form of doubts. I start doubting myself. If I do not pay attention to these thoughts they may become habitual and they may well turn into beliefs. *"I am not able to make progress doing this work." "I am not good enough."* These are limiting beliefs and if they remain unchallenged they will become rules for me. Forming these beliefs will lower the potential for my pain in not achieving progress. They will also lower my potential for getting my life the way that I want it.

By employing mindfulness we are able to identify feelings of discomfort. We are able to identify the thoughts that are creating these feelings of discomfort. When we are mindful of our thinking we can spot doubts, we can see them as communication from our saboteur. We can intercept them and challenge them before they become beliefs for us, before they start limiting us and become rules in our life.

Likewise with progress being so important for me there are other dangers. What happens when I take a few days off or a holiday? If I am not careful my saboteur is going to get agitated:

Why is he not trying to make progress? He is not going to make progress lying on the beach or playing golf. Send him some messages to get him back to work.

I am happily lying on the beach and what happens? I start getting restless. I start feeling guilty about relaxing. I start getting thoughts like, *"I really should check my emails at some stage."* *"I had better start getting prepared to go back to work."* Thank you very much saboteur!

Fortunately for me this does not happen. Here is the reason: my interpretation of the value of progress is that it involves progress at work but also progress in my personal development, progress in my contribution to others, progress in being mindful, progress in spending time in being mode. By being mindful that my progress is not limited to my work I can happily spend a week on the beach without being bothered too much by my saboteur. I send the message to my saboteur that *"All is well. I am relaxing this week, recharging my batteries. I will be back to making progress next week."*

Mind filtering and mindfulness

The deletion, distortion and generalisation that goes on in our mind filtering unit determines our interpretation of our experiences. The filtering takes the form of applying memories, decisions, judgements, values, beliefs, and rules to the information that we take in through our senses, and this leaves us with internal representations of what we are seeing, hearing, feeling, tasting and smelling. Based on these internal representations we will form a state of mind, and we will behave in a certain way.

There are essentially three stages to this process:
1) Receiving the information through our senses
2) Filtering and processing the information
3) Ending up with a state of mind and some resulting behaviour.

We have no influence over the first part of the process. Two people in the same situation receive the same bits of information. The thing that will determine the reality for these two people is in the second part of the process. Dependent upon their mind filtering, they may get very different results for themselves. The second part of the process is performed by our unconscious mind, and as we know, we condition or programme our unconscious mind with our conscious thinking.

We are therefore able to determine our state of mind and our resulting behaviour by making an intervention at stage two of the process. As we are constantly processing so much information, we do not always have time to become consciously aware of our filtering as it occurs.

We can use our mindfulness sessions and exercises to examine our thinking and explore our judgements, beliefs and rules thus making sure that our mind filters are set up the way that we want them. As we become aware of the doubts that we have, the false beliefs that we have established, the limiting decisions that we have made, so we get in touch with their creator, our saboteur. We are able to befriend and challenge our saboteur. This has the impact of changing our mind filters, our unconscious processes, allowing us to make better decisions, get better behaviours, and improved results.

Rules, decisions and beliefs

We live life by a set of rules that we hold in our unconscious mind. We accumulate these rules throughout life:

- We adopt other people's rules as well as their values. In the same way as values, many of our rules originate from our family, friends, teachers and other people through the media.
- We accumulate rules by making decisions based upon our interpretation of events and the feedback that we receive from our saboteur.

Some of these rules support us and others hinder us. In common with all behaviour we adopt rules with a positive intention but sometimes they can have the reverse effect.

We treat our rules as facts. They become facts for us when we decide to adopt them. The thing is that they are not necessarily actual facts, but we adopt them as such.

Here is an example of the unconscious process of adopting rules:

- When we are young, a parent says to us "You should always be punctual."
- We examine this belief consciously as we digest what our parent says.
- We have no reason or evidence to doubt it, so we put it on our list of possible rules.
- We spend time examining events as they occur to see if the possible rule is fact.
- We see someone running for a bus and missing it. They look really frustrated.
- We associate their frustration with not being punctual. Our unconscious mind makes the link back to what our parent told us.
- "You should always be punctual" becomes a rule for us. We assume it as a fact.

It is quite possible that we then spend our entire life living by this rule without ever challenging it. It is not a fact, it is a belief. Logically thinking we now know that it is not a fact because it is possible to have the opposite view.

In this case, the rule may generally support us, but it may not always be the case, sometimes it may cause us problems:

- If we go through a stage in life where we are really busy and this affects our punctuality, then we may become really disappointed and frustrated, we may even feel guilty when we keep breaking our rule.

- If we have a partner who does not have the same belief and being punctual is not important to them, then this could cause a great deal of tension between us.

We may never be able to identify why we are feeling disappointed, frustrated, guilty, annoyed with our partner. In fact we may not even recognise what the exact feelings are, we may just feel uncomfortable and irritable, agitated. It is possible that we never trace these feelings back to our rule and challenge that rule because our rules are unconscious.

Beliefs are what we hold to be true, they are our rules.

- We receive suggestions from other people, our unconscious mind spots patterns in events and we receive suggestions from our saboteur.
- These suggestions including our doubts go on our "possible rules list".
- We then unconsciously seek evidence that the possible rules are true.
- Something happens that confirms our doubt or appears to confirm the suggestion.
- We make a decision. The doubt, the suggestion, the belief is true. It becomes a rule.

Rules that we hold unconsciously remain rules for us until we challenge them or until we come across evidence that appears to contradict them. Hopefully, most of our rules will be supporting us but we also will hold rules that are causing us problems, or outdated rules that are simply no longer relevant for us.

In times of stress, when we are dealing with lots of bits of information we tend to rely more and more on unconscious processes, we are less likely to challenge our rules and beliefs. In times like this our saboteur is on high alert and is offering us lots of escape routes, in the form of doubts, and it is encouraging us to make limiting decisions. Once we make a decision, we make our rules and sometimes they can last a lifetime.

Mindfulness allows us to step back, take a different perspective, take a breathing space. In this breathing space, and as we examine our thinking and our feelings, the sensations in our body, we are able to make conscious the rules that are driving our feelings and behaviour. As we bring awareness to them, we challenge our rules, we challenge our beliefs, we challenge our saboteur.

In the example above, we made a decision in an instant about the rule, "You should always be punctual." Our rules are often made like this, based on weak, circumstantial and possibly inaccurate assumptions. The first stage in changing rules is to become aware of them: this is what mindfulness will assist us in doing.

Once we have identified the problem we can then identify the decision that created the rule. We can go back to the decision in our mind's eye and challenge the decision, thus altering the memory of the decision and changing the rule.

Here are some of the most common destructive rules that originate from the saboteur and that in times of stress we adopt as fact for ourselves:

- I can't stop worrying about what other people think of me
- I can't control my anger
- I can't make my relationship work
- I must never fail
- I must be strong
- I can't give up
- I wish I were somewhere else
- I can't motivate myself
- I can't make decisions
- I must never let people down
- There must be something wrong with me
- I can't stop thinking negative thoughts
- I am the only one who can do this
- Something has to change
- I mustn't wait a minute

How many of these are rules that you have adopted for yourself? What other rules can you add to this list that are true for you?

Take the belief: "There must be something wrong with me." I hear people say this all the time. At some point in time people who hold this belief must have thought "I wonder if there is something wrong with me?" They will have held this thought in the back of their mind until something happened that led them to decide that it is true. This could be someone else saying "There is something wrong with you." Or it could be some form of "evidence" that led them to conclude that it must be true. Either way, the chances are that they made the decision based on unqualified evidence.

None of these beliefs have to be true. They are not objective facts. They are beliefs that your saboteur wants you to adopt in a misguided effort to protect you. You could equally come across evidence that leads you to adopt the opposite belief and hold that to be true instead. It is just at stress points in our life we listen to our saboteur and to other people and at these times we do not have the resources to challenge them.

Challenging beliefs

One way to challenge beliefs is to go back to the decision that made the rule in the first place and re-examine the evidence.

Ask yourself: "When did I decide that?"

You may or you may not remember specifically when it was or exactly what caused the decision. It doesn't matter if you do not consciously remember, we are not after a conscious response. Change takes place at the unconscious level. So go ahead and ask your unconscious mind. You may get an inkling of when it was or a signal.

Examine the decision. What was your evidence? Is it possible that you were incorrect and made the wrong decision?

For example. "When did I decide that there must be something wrong with me? I think it was when I was really busy and started forgetting simple things. After work one day I went straight home and completely forgot that I had arranged to meet my wife and children at my parents house. Hmmm. Thinking about that now, I can understand that I was really preoccupied with work at the time and just wasn't thinking. There isn't anything wrong with me. It could happen to anyone." Belief removed.

Go ahead and write out any beliefs that you have that you think may be holding you back. Examine them in this way.

Noticing silence, sounds, and thoughts

How easy did you find it to come up with a list of beliefs? It is not always easy and the reason for this is that beliefs are largely unconscious. We have rules but just like our values we do not necessarily go around thinking about them all the time. They are like an undercurrent in our life, they operate in the background.

One way to discover our limiting beliefs is through being mindful in and of our thinking. By noticing our thoughts when we receive them we can start to examine them. Rather than it seeming like constant noise in the background we can actually start making out the tune that our daily thoughts are playing.

In this exercise we are going to pay specific attention to silence, sounds and thoughts. Just like our thoughts, sounds around us often go unnoticed. We pay attention to them unconsciously and we process them on autopilot. In fact there are several similarities between sounds and thoughts:

- Sounds and thoughts come out of nowhere.
- We have no control over either the sounds or the thoughts that we receive.
- We can choose the level of attention that we pay to either of them.
- We often process sounds and thoughts unconsciously, as if on

autopilot.
- They can both affect us emotionally as they act as triggers for our emotions.

If we pay attention in any moment in time, sounds arise out of nowhere. Just listen now. What can you hear? Sounds of nature, vehicles, other machinery, movements of other people, voices of other people? None of these sounds are predictable, none are within your control.

Sounds, just like thoughts form some of the eleven million bits of information that we are exposed to every second. Our unconscious mind filters out most of the sounds and handles most of the thoughts without bothering the conscious mind as it judges that there are more important pieces of information for the conscious mind to be concerned with. This is the reason why most sounds pass us by unnoticed and why most thoughts are processed unconsciously.

We can train our unconscious mind to allow us greater awareness of our thoughts so that we can identify the beliefs, rules and decisions that are underpinning our behaviour. We do that via these mindfulness exercises.

In this exercise we observe the similarities between sounds and thoughts, bring them into our conscious attention. We break the process down to two parts. Receiving and noticing.

Without sound we have silence. Without thought, there is silence inside. We receive sound. Unconsciously we either decide to pay attention to it or let it go unnoticed. If the sound is really loud, then we have no choice but to pay attention to it in the first instance. For one thing it will awaken our saboteur. Until the source of the sound is identified we may feel fear. We notice the sound. We can then relate the sound to things that we have heard in the past and we can then provide it with a label and a possible identity. If the sound is nothing to worry about, then the message goes back to our saboteur, *all is normal*. Our saboteur goes back to rest, the feeling of fear dissolves.

With thoughts, the process is similar. We can learn to pay attention to receiving thoughts. We can consciously notice the thought. Consciously noticing thoughts will lead to us labeling the thoughts. E.g. "This is planning." "This is worrying." "This is a limiting belief." Etc. We can identify the involvement of our saboteur in the process and once we have identified and labeled the thought, then we can choose what to do next: watch the thought dissolve, or send a message to our saboteur to challenge the thought.

Silence, Sounds and Thoughts - Me-Time Exercise 4

Preparation

This exercise is best conducted in a sitting position. Sit upright with a straight spine. Relax your shoulders and neck. Close your eyes.

Settle by getting in touch with your breathing. Notice your breath going in and out of your body. Pay attention to each in-breath and each out-breath. Once you are feeling settled then expand your attention to your whole body. Breathe in and notice the air filling your body. Breathe out and notice the air leaving your body. Notice the sensations in your body as you breathe.

Spend a couple of minutes being mindful of your breath and your body. Re-awaken the anchor that links your breath to the present moment. Be mindful that you can use this anchor at any time during this exercise to bring your attention back to the present should you become distracted.

Sounds and silence

When you are ready, start directing your attention to your hearing. There is no need to strive in any way to hear certain things, just pay attention to any sounds that you are receiving naturally.

Just as scenery has a landscape, so do sounds. There are many things that make up the landscape of sounds. Become open to noticing this landscape, be receptive to it.

Notice how some sounds are more prominent than others, they borrow your attention. Just listen to them arise and disappear. Notice any gaps in between the sounds. Notice that they have a definite beginning and end and that in between, there is relative silence.

As you remain open and receptive you may notice how you label the sounds. Birds, insects, wind, cars, aircraft, creaking water pipes, voices, movement. Once you have noticed the label, just go back to the pure experience of noticing the sound. Notice the quality in the sound, the loudness, the pitch, the duration.

Notice when your attention moves away from the sounds. You may find that you attach pictures in your mind's eye to the sounds, imagining how they are being produced, what is producing them. If you do, then just revert to hearing the sound itself. Notice any thoughts that creep in. Make note of what the thoughts are, then revert your attention to receiving and noticing the ebbing and flowing of the sounds.

Carry on paying attention to sounds for four minutes or so.

Thoughts and silence of mind

Move your spotlight of attention now to your thoughts. See them as clouds approaching, moving through, retreating, dissolving.

Pay attention to your thoughts in the same way as you were paying attention to the sounds. Notice them appearing, notice how you can label them. Notice how, when you continue to pay attention to them you can sense them leaving, dissolving in the light of your attention.

Again, there is no need to strive to notice your thoughts, just pay attention to them as they arrive in your consciousness. Let them ebb and flow. Notice the gaps between your thoughts, the silence.

You can pay attention to your thoughts as if they are on stage in your mind. Just as you can look up to the sky and see clouds, large and small, so you can observe your thoughts. Notice the pieces of blue sky between the clouds: these are the gaps between your thoughts. As you pay more and more attention to the blue sky, so your clouds may shrink, dissolve and disperse.

You could see your thoughts as a slideshow playing in your mind. Each thought is a different slide. Some thoughts are still, some animated. As you sit there looking at the screen in your mind, watching your slideshow, notice the gaps in between the slides. Notice as the slides change: are you doing that or is it happening all of its own accord?

Pay attention to how your thoughts may want to drag you in. How they may set off a chain of thoughts. How it may be possible, as you get dragged in, to start feeling emotions associated to the thoughts. Step back a bit and imagine looking at yourself watching the slideshow. Notice how any emotion dissolves with the thoughts as the slides change in your mind.

Be playful as you observe. Experiment with just playing the role of the observer, watching thoughts as they appear and disappear. Notice the qualities in your thoughts. Are there images? Are they movies or stills? Are they in black and white or are they in colour? Are there sounds attached to them? What feelings and emotions do they have associated with them?

Which thoughts, clouds or slides could you attribute to your saboteur?

At any time you can use your breathing anchor to pull you away from your thoughts and back to the present moment. Notice how you can use this. Experiment with using it, then sit back and enjoy the slideshow.

Summary of Silence, Sounds and Thoughts - Me-Time Exercise 4 (10 mins)

1) Sit upright with relaxed shoulders and neck. Close your eyes.
2) Get in touch with your breathing.
3) As you breathe, notice the air filling and leaving your body. Notice any sensations in your body. (2 Mins)
4) Start paying attention to your hearing. (4 Mins)
5) Observe your landscape of sounds.
6) Notice the sounds arriving and disappearing. Notice the silence between the sounds.
7) Pay attention to your labeling of the sounds.
8) Notice the quality in the sounds, the loudness, the pitch, the duration.
9) Move the spotlight of your attention to your thoughts. (4 Mins)
10) Notice any thoughts arriving and dissolving like clouds. Notice their ebb and flow.
11) Observe any gaps in thinking as if blue sky between clouds.
12) See your thoughts as a slideshow. Notice what is on the slides in your mind. What pictures, sounds, feelings are there? What are the fine details of the representation in your mind's eye?
13) Be playful. Which thoughts could you attribute to your saboteur?
14) What emotions, if any, are in your thoughts? Do the thoughts drag you in? Do they keep replaying? Do they set off any chain of other thoughts?

It is impossible to label something that you are not familiar with. This is the reason that we have been building up layers in your familiarity with your thinking. The first stage is to become aware of your thinking. Your unconscious mind will then set about making connections, seeing patterns that will allow you to start recognising your thinking and labeling your thoughts.

If we first of all see our thoughts as clouds in the sky, we can then start identifying patterns in the clouds, the colour of them, the thickness of them, the size of them and the gaps in between. This is how we can see the involvement of our saboteur, our limiting decisions, our limiting beliefs, our emotional and psychological fears.

Peter explains his experience. "At first my thoughts just seemed to me like congestion in my mind. I knew that I was thinking but I was not able to identify exactly what the content of the thoughts were. It helped to think of them as clouds as it enabled me to start seeing them as separate events rather than just a storm."

Joyce said. "Playing the role of observer was useful for me. I realised that I could observe my thoughts without getting entangled in them. I got a sense of them being there. I could associate pictures with them and what I noticed was that as I kept on watching them as slides on a screen they would tend to just drop off the screen."

Playing the observer to your thoughts allows you to get some distance from them. When you have distance so you gain perspective. This has the benefit of allowing you to look at them more objectively, as if from outside the thought rather than getting involved in a thinking system that provokes feelings and a chain of other events.

Normally, when we experience a thought we do so unconsciously. This allows our unconscious mind the freedom to make connections and associations with the thought. Making the connections to previous thoughts and memories often leads to this chain or cycle of linked thoughts, some of which may carry emotions. Unconsciously we pluck the emotion out of our unconscious and pull it through into the present moment.

By observing our thoughts and keeping distance from them so we make them conscious. This intercepts the unconscious mind from making the associations, thus breaking the cycle and leaving us free of the emotion.

Did you notice the involvement of your saboteur in any of your thoughts? "I had to chuckle to myself." Peter said. "I was looking out for my thoughts and nothing was there. I just had silence, blue skies. Then out of nowhere I noticed that I was thinking about some work related things that I had to do after the exercise. I realised that this was my saboteur at play. Then I noticed that I was actually judging the tasks that I had to do, *'I haven't got time to do that'* sprang to mind as a thought. I chuckled as it dawned on me that this was also my saboteur sending me a message. *'It's ok. Plenty of time,'* I found myself replying. The thought disappeared."

The more you look out for thoughts the more you are actually paying attention to now. This is sometimes why it takes a few moments for your thoughts to appear. Be patient though because they will not be far away! Observe your thoughts and you will see planning, worrying, future and past thinking, the doing mode. As you examine these thoughts, what judgements do you see? Is there any emotion involved? Do you get any creeping feeling of unease? Look out for your saboteur. When you notice it, then see if you can spot any untruths in the thought, any possible assumptions, any underlying fear. Reassure your saboteur. "Thanks for letting me know. It's going to be ok." Watch the thought retreat, the feeling ease.

Notice how, when you resist something it gets stronger. If you are hearing something that you do not like, then it takes over your consciousness, makes life unpleasant for you. If you push thoughts away, then they come back stronger and with more emotion. Rather than resisting them, just letting sounds and thoughts be and noticing them keeps you from allowing them to take your consciousness away from you. You can judge them from a distance, let them fade into the background or act accordingly.

Habit Breaker 4 - Painting a picture

If you are not an artist, then when was the last time that you painted a picture? It was probably some time ago. Painting can be a very therapeutic activity, a very mindful activity.

You will need some watercolour paints, a couple of small brushes, a blank piece of paper and a subject to paint. You can choose anything to paint: your partner, a friend, a piece of fruit, a flower or any other object.

As you prepare to paint, really pay attention to your subject. Notice that it is lighter where the light shines on it and darker where there are shadows. Get a sense of the scale of the subject and the colours that you will need.

Notice as you paint how you get absorbed into the process. It does not matter what your painting looks like. Have fun and be playful. Be gentle with yourself. Notice when you are beginning to judge your outcome. Let it be. Enjoy the experience.

Key Points

- When we become mindful of our thinking, then we are able to manage our saboteur.
- Mindfulness helps us identify our doubts and limiting decisions that become our rules. These are often born from our unconscious mind fulfilling its duty to protect us. In reality they do not protect us, they limit us, they are a form of self sabotage.
- As we become aware of our thoughts so we can identify those

automatic unconscious thought patterns that hold us back. We can use this awareness to make more empowering decisions, eliminate our doubts and create rules that support us in living a happier and more successful life.

- Once we have identified any decisions or rules that we have that may be holding us back, we can challenge them. Just ask: "When did I decide that?" Examine the decision in a new light.
- Thoughts come to us out of nowhere, as do sounds. In the Silence, Sounds and Thoughts Me-Time exercise we experiment with paying mindful attention to sounds around us in order to start improving our awareness of how they manifest, how we register them in our consciousness and what thoughts that we generate about them. This builds our skill in observing our thoughts and how we place judgements on things.
- Notice the landscape of thoughts and sounds that make up your experience in the moment. See your thoughts as a slideshow, watch the slides changing all of their own accord. Notice that we can label the slides as they pass by. We have the ability to see our thoughts as events rather than being part of us. When we do this we are able to be more objective and dissociate from them, thus resolving the emotions within them.

CHAPTER 20

Accepting and befriending your saboteur

Whatever our current circumstances in life, however we see our future we are not going to make things any better by resisting them. In fact if we resist things then we can make the situation a whole lot worse and feel really unhappy.

Resistance is a completely natural reaction to things that we do not want. If we foresee something occurring in our life that we judge as being bad, then we tend to react in one of two ways. Fight or flight. We try to work out a solution, or we ignore it and hope that it doesn't happen.

Sometimes, however things happen and we are powerless to do anything about them. When the outcome to something is out of our control then resisting that thing can only cause us to feel more anxious and unhappy.

Take the example of noise. If our next door neighbour decides to have some extensive building work done, then we are going to have a period of time when, if we are in our house during the day, it will be noisy. We can expect builders to arrive at 8am, turn on the radio and use loud machinery on and off all the way through to 5pm. In this situation we have a choice: we can accept that there is going to be noise during the day for a while, or we can let it bother us.

The natural first instinct is to try to find a solution. What can we do about it? Can we tell them to keep the noise down? No, not really. Can we wear earplugs all day long? No, this is not practical. Can we pack a suitcase and go on holiday for a few months? For most of us, this solution is unfortunately out of reach.

When we realise that there is no solution, then we feel trapped. This is an awful feeling, we want to escape, but there is nowhere to escape to. We can try and ignore the fact that the builders are on their way, maybe they will not make any noise. However, let's face facts, the noise is on its way, it is inevitable.

We can then spend the next few months resenting the fact that our neighbour is having the work done or we can accept it and cease our resistance. If we choose to spend our time resenting things; then we can resent our neighbours for having the work done, we can resent the builder's for making the noise, we can resent the noise itself. Every time we notice the builders radio, the dust, the noise from the machinery we can complain about it to ourselves or anyone else who is listening, and we will feel thoroughly miserable. In fact, we can start the resenting process by just thinking about the situation in the future. Most people in this situation spend some time resenting things before they eventually get fed up with resenting, realise that they are making themselves unhappy, possibly unwell, and decide that they will just have to accept it.

Frankly we should save ourselves the time and the misery. If there are things in our life that are not the way that we want them but we are not able immediately to do anything about them, then the best way to respond is to drop our resistance and accept them for what they are. Watch out for the reaction of your saboteur to this statement. You may be thinking "I couldn't possibly just sit back and accept things like this." You can, it comes down to your rules, decisions and beliefs again.

We are not talking about accepting the unacceptable. If someone is taking advantage of your good nature, bullying you, then we are not talking about lying down and letting them walk all over you like a doormat. If this is the case, then you need to stand up for yourself. This is when the fight or flight response is useful for us.

We are also not talking about giving up or giving in. There are certain rules in life, principles, that you have adopted and that work for you, that you see as part of your make-up. If someone or something breaches one of those rules then you may find their behaviour or the situation intolerable. We are not suggesting that you give up on the fight for your principles.

What we are saying is, relinquish the inner resistance. Reconcile with your resentment. Can you do something about the situation in this moment in time? If not, then when can you do something about it? Up until that moment let go of the resentment, let go of your inner resistance to that thing. When you let go of your resistance it sends a message to your saboteur: "It's ok." Your saboteur will rest in the knowledge that it has done its job.

As long as you cling on to resentment and resist things, this also sends a message to your saboteur. "This is not over. This is not what I want. I am unhappy with this." You saboteur will respond by reminding you of how frustrated you are, how angry you are, how unhappy you are at every opportunity. You will get repeated negative thoughts, chains of negative thoughts.

This may seem like a tricky principle to get hold of at first. The key to it is to become mindful of every moment. If you remove judgement, then every moment in time is an opportunity to embrace life. When we did the Silence, sounds and thoughts exercise in the last chapter we listened out for the various sounds that we could hear in any one moment. We listened to the sounds as sounds, rather than judging them. At any time there are lots of sounds that we can normally choose to listen to. We tend to hear the loudest sound as this is the one that pulls at our attention. However if we choose to, after we have registered it in our consciousness, we can ignore the loudest sound, listen through that sound and examine the other sounds. In this case what happens to the loudest sound? It is still there but it fades into the background doesn't it? We can choose how important different sounds are to us by which ones we direct our attention to.

This is the same with thinking. The thoughts that we direct attention to are the thoughts that we give energy to. We can choose to see our thoughts as events, clouds and watch them pass by, or we can get embroiled in them and set off a chain of thoughts and feelings.

Of course there are some things in life that do not pass by in a moment, some things persist. Take ill health for example. If we become seriously ill, then there may be a stage that we reach where there are no further solutions available to us. To our conscious mind this is unacceptable, however there is nothing that we can do about it. No amount of problem solving thoughts will help. Most people in this situation will do one of two things: continue to resist, to fight reality, or to pretend that it is not happening and hope that nothing comes of it.

As far as health is concerned I believe that there is always room for hope. There are too many amazing stories of recovery and survival for us to concede defeat to any disease. The billions of neurological links in our body allowing communication of thoughts throughout our system encourage us to keep believing that the seemingly impossible is possible, recovery is possible.

We must never give in to a disease, always believe that we will recover but we must drop our resistance to the moment. Each moment is a separate moment in time. We see a moment in time as good or bad by adding our judgement to it. In actual fact a moment in time is never good or bad, it just is as it is. We tend to judge the present moment based on past and future events. If we are seriously ill, then it is natural to us to see the present moment as being really bad, but we do have a choice over this judgement. We have a choice as to whether to place a judgment on the moment, and we have a choice over what that judgement is.

If we are mindful of every moment, then we become mindful of our judgements in and of every moment. It is possible for us to be seriously ill and to embrace the present moment, enjoying the external sensory experience, enjoying the company of others, enjoying nature.

Mindfulness suggests that we approach our difficulties rather than shying away from them. Rather than ignoring the fact that we may be seriously ill, we can contemplate this fact without placing judgement on it. By contemplating it we are approaching it, getting to know it. We can explore the possible consequences, recovery or death again without placing judgement on them. Whilst relinquishing our need to judge and resist the moment, we retain our resolve to recover from our illness. This is the acceptance that we are talking about. Resolve and determination to achieve the outcomes that you want in life but acceptance of the present moment.

Whatever we resist in life we unconsciously give our permission to persist. Awareness is acceptance. With awareness we are able to make better decisions and choices. With choices and better decisions we get better results.

We create our own reality. We cannot alter what happens to us but we can determine how we react to things and judge them.

Exploring Resistance and Difficulties - Me-Time Exercise 5 (10 Minutes)

Preparation

Find somewhere comfortable to sit where you will remain undisturbed for ten minutes. Start by noticing your breathing and then move your attention on to your body as a whole. When you are feeling relaxed and connected with the exercise move your attention on to sounds and your thoughts.

Observing painful thoughts or difficulties

As you are observing your thoughts notice if your attention is pulling you away from your breath and your body into any difficulties that you are experiencing in life. In terms of difficulties, it could be any type of painful thoughts, feelings or emotions.

Rather than letting these thoughts drift on by we are going to spend some time in this exercise examining them. We are going to leave the thoughts on the screen and explore the slides.

As you observe your thoughts, and if one of these thoughts makes an appearance, then just let the thought take place. Become aware of what you are thinking. Then take your awareness into your body, notice if there are any sensations taking place that are associated with this thought. Are there any emotions there?

If you discover any sensations, then gently shift your attention to the part of your body where you feel the sensations. Breathe into the sensation on an in-breath and breathe out of it on the out-breath.

You are not attempting to change or alter the sensations, just exploring them. As you explore them, bear in mind that they probably have some saboteur involvement with them, so just gently reassure yourself, "it's all ok. I'm just checking this out. It's ok to feel this sensation, I just want to learn more about it."

Hold your awareness of the sensation in your mind. Stay with this sensation. Notice what your mind is doing with it. Are you trying to change it? Or are you just exploring it with your attention and breath?

If you find that there are no painful thoughts that spring to mind all of their own accord, then see if you can deliberately bring to mind a minor difficulty that you are having in your life at the moment. Something that is unresolved. This may be a disagreement with someone, an argument that you have had, something that you are finding yourself worrying about, something that is making you feel uncomfortable, guilty, or angry.

Hold that thing in mind and as you do that switch your attention to your body and notice what sensations are there. Notice if you can relate the sensations in your body to the thoughts that you are having. Approach the sensations playfully, explore them. Breathe into the sensations and out of the sensations. Without striving to change anything, notice any shift in the sensations. If and when you need to, as you approach the sensation you can give your saboteur some reassurance. "This is going to be ok. Let me explore it."

Let your attention and awareness rest with the sensations as you explore them, breathing around and into them, noticing how they seem to soften as you breathe out of them. Just let them be, accept them and observe how they change all on their own. Let go of any tension that you feel around the sensations with your out-breaths.

When you realise that the sensations have softened a little and no longer hold the same pull on your attention then gently shift your attention back to your breath and thought watching again.

Continue for ten minutes.

Summary of Exploring Resistance and Difficulties - Me-Time Exercise 5 (10 mins)

1) Sit comfortably and notice your breathing.
2) Let your awareness rest with your breathing and your body.
3) Move your awareness to sounds and thoughts.
4) Notice any painful thoughts or difficulties that come to mind.
5) If none spring to mind, then think of a situation in your life where you are experiencing difficulties and watch your thoughts about that.
6) Let the thoughts rest in your mind's eye.
7) Notice any sensations in your body that may be linked to these thoughts.
8) Approach the sensations playfully. Explore them. Breathe into and out of them.
9) Resist the temptation to fix anything. Just continue to breathe in and out of the sensations. Let the out-breath soften them if it wants to.
10) Reassure your saboteur. "It's going to be ok. I just want to explore."
11) As the sensation softens and leaves your attention bring your focus back to your breath and your thought watching.
12) Continue for ten minutes.

During these mindfulness exercises we have been layering in your understanding of your thinking and how it relates to the sensations in your body. When we use our awareness to go in search of sensations, then they may at first be hard to define. We are not necessarily looking out for pain. Most sensations related to difficulties and fear take the form of some kind of discomfort. We may feel tension or tightness of some form or another. Pleasant sensations may just take the form of a sense of ease, softness, a gentle hum, or a light buzzing. Whatever you experience and whatever you feel is ok for these exercises. Breathe into the pleasant feelings to energise them. Breathe into and out of your discomfort to soften it.

You will not be absolutely sure that you are making the right connection between a thought and a sensation. This is ok too. With practice you are learning to trust your unconscious mind to make the connections for you and provide you with the signals to bring that connection to your awareness.

As you approach the things that you are resisting, as you breathe into the sensations that you discover, as they sense your awareness embracing them, no longer are you storing up the emotions that are involved with them. You are embracing the emotions, you are embracing your saboteur. Darkness cannot exist wherever light shines. Shine the light of your awareness on your difficulties and your problems and the darkness, gloom and resistance inside dissolve.

Continue to practise approaching, exploring and embracing your difficulties and you start installing a powerful autopilot for yourself. Your unconscious mind will follow your instructions, it will make the necessary connections, and it will understand better what you want more of in your life. It will release you of your stored up negative emotions.

As I used this technique to explore my own difficulties, I started to feel almost a palpable sense of release sweeping over me. Almost as though my body was saying "Thanks for paying attention. I can let go of all that baggage now."

I found it really useful to keep reassuring myself that "It is ok to feel this. It is ok to think this way." It seemed as though it was saying to my saboteur, "You can relax my friend. You are just doing your job, I understand that. I am not ignoring you anymore I am listening to you. You do not need to stay on such high alert. I am paying attention." The response was that I felt at peace with myself.

As I have continued to practise mindfulness, this peace has remained. I do still get annoyed and frustrated. I do still get that uncomfortable feeling that for me sits in the pit of my stomach, but it doesn't last long. I do still occasionally wake up in the middle of the night with worries creeping up on me, as they do with everyone, but now my worries are short lived, they never start getting into the system to cause a problem and they are soon replaced with peace inside as my saboteur settles down and lets me sleep.

Practising mindful acceptance releases us from our chains of negative thoughts. Once we have addressed and accepted our difficulty, then the unconscious mind learns that it no longer needs to feed us with further associated negative thoughts. By exploring our difficulties this allows us to become aware of the accuracy of our thoughts. In this way we become aware of any limiting beliefs and rules that we hold that do not support us.

We only remain trapped by our fears as long as we ignore them. If we approach and explore them, then we embrace them and they lose their power over us. This is how we will get our life the way that we want it.

Key Points

- When life does not go our way or when we have a perception of difficulties looming in our future, then we tend to build up resistances to these things in our thoughts. We wish that things were different. We wrestle with the truth in our minds, seeking some kind of solution. When the solution is not immediately obvious, then we may experience a sustained period of negativity in our thoughts as we feel trapped by our circumstances.
- The solution is to accept each and every moment on its own merit.
- We follow an exercise to bring awareness to the things that we are resisting and to approach our difficulties. This is the way that we will befriend our saboteur and gain acceptance,

giving us inner peace.
- Through this exercise we notice sensations in our body. We approach them with our breathing and our awareness. We explore them. We breathe into them to soften them. This is how we lessen our resistance and how we learn acceptance.

CHAPTER 21

Being compassionate

It is time to start being a bit nicer to yourself. I don't just mean spoiling yourself by booking a spa weekend, although that could be a very mindful and relaxing experience. I mean start being nice to yourself in a more general sense.

Whilst many of us can be very defensive when we feel that we are being criticised, picked on and insulted by other people, we are never shy of giving ourselves a whole load of put-downs, negative feedback, even abuse.

We provide our own feedback and criticism via our self talk. "You are looking old today. Just look at those wrinkles!" How would you react if someone else said that to you? Just imagine what impact saying this to yourself as you look in the mirror has on your self image and self respect and self worth. Just imagine what messages you are sending out via your internal neural networks. After saying this, it would be no surprise at all if you were feeling tired and zapped of energy by the end of the day, would it?

Your unconscious mind takes your self talk personally. It takes it as an instruction and passes it on to the body via the neural networks. So, watch out for the messages that you are sending via your self talk!

We find it really tricky to listen to negative feedback about ourselves from other people and yet we spend so much of our time indulging in personal put-downs. It can have a really negative effect on our self image.

Here are some of the common pieces of self criticism that float around in our heads and our self talk:

- I am so stupid at times
- I am ugly
- I am no good at this
- I have no self control
- You idiot!
- You just do not learn do you?
- If I try I am only going to mess it up
- I will only do it wrong
- I am useless at this
- Nobody likes me
- What is the matter with me?

How many of these statements and other similar ones have you aimed at yourself over the years? The statement: "What is the matter with me?" Implies that something is the matter, something is wrong and this is the origin of a limiting belief. This message sends the unconscious mind off in search of something that it could possibly identify as being a problem with you. Eventually it will probably find the evidence to back up the implied suggestion. The belief "There is something the matter with me" is therefore born.

Some of the criticisms are directed straight at ourselves, "I am so stupid" and some criticisms are directed as if to a third party "You idiot!" It is as if the "You" that we are referring to is someone else. Either way, the result is the same, our unconscious mind takes the criticism personally. It learns "I am stupid and I am an idiot."

You would not say these things to your best friend, would you? So, why is it ok to say these things to yourself?

We act according to our self image, and our level of self worth. All of these self criticisms affect our self image. If we keep telling ourselves that "nobody likes me" eventually we will start believing it and we will start behaving accordingly. We will start developing behaviours that fit this image of ourselves as being unlikeable. If we believe that "I am unlikeable" then what is the point in trying to be likeable? We stop trying and so develop unwanted and unappealing behaviour patterns. It is a self fulfilling cycle.

When we persist in delivering these self criticisms then we end up believing that they are true. If we do not value our own self worth, then there is a significant danger that we will even start believing that "we are not worthy." Not worthy of other people's love. Not worthy of praise, either from ourselves or other people. We end up falling out of love for ourselves. This can lead to self destructive behaviour such as overeating, drinking too much alcohol, drug abuse, other forms of self harm.

Start recognising the value of positive self talk. Start breaking the cycles of self criticism by becoming aware of any negative self talk or 'coaching' that you are giving yourself. Use the exercises to observe any negative self talk that appears in your thinking.

It is time for you to start being more compassionate towards yourself. We are going to explore and develop this in the next exercise.

Compassion to Self and Others - Me-Time Exercise 6 (10 Minutes)

Preparation

Find a comfortable place to rest, relax and stay alert for the duration of this exercise. You can sit or lie down, whichever suits you best.

Start by noticing your breathing. Gather your breath and start paying attention to the breath entering and leaving your body. Focus your attention on the whole of your body and your breath.

Thoughts

When the first thoughts start pulling on your attention start watching them. Notice how, as a result of your practice so far, you have a definite choice: you can observe the thoughts, or you can return your attention to your breathing and your body.

Pay attention to thoughts coming into your consciousness. Explore the thoughts. Notice any sensations in your body. Explore the connection between the thoughts and the sensations. Breathe into and out of the sensations. Notice the thoughts dissolve or move on through your mind. Watch them leave. Bring your attention back to your body and breath.

Pebbles of compassion

After a few minutes of thought watching and returning to body and breath, bring to mind a still lake on a sunny day. Imagine your body and mind as this still lake. Notice how, when thoughts pass by they create ripples in the lake. Let the lake become still again.

As you hold this in mind I want you to think of the following instructions:

- *May I be healthy and strong*
- *May I be happy*
- *May I be filled with ease*

(Choose different words if you like. Choose words that embody the way that you want to lead your life, the way that you want your life to be.)

See each one of these statements as a pebble. One by one, and as gently as you like you are going to drop the pebbles into your lake.

Pick up the first pebble, and drop it into your lake. *"May I be healthy and strong."* Watch the ripples on the lake as the after-effects of the impact of the pebble take place. As you do this, notice any affect in your body, in your thoughts. Notice any feelings, or sensations that arise.

Repeat the process with your other two pebbles.

When you feel ready, go on to the next step.

Compassion for others

Bring to mind someone that is close to you, a loved one. Wish them well using the same statements.

As you think of that person and hold them in mind, just say to them *"may you be healthy and strong."* Watch for any reaction in your body. Explore this reaction. Notice any judgements. Take your time. Pause a little.

"May you be happy." Pay attention to any reaction. Pause. Breathe.
"May you be filled with ease." Pay attention to any reaction. Breathe.

Now bring to mind a stranger. Someone who you do not know well but someone who you can picture in your mind's eye. It may be someone who you have occasional contact with.

As you hold them in mind, give them the same statements and notice your reaction in your body. Breathe all the while.

Next, bring to mind someone with whom you may have been

having certain difficulties recently. Follow the same process. Notice how that makes you feel. Explore how it makes you feel.

If you feel any distress at any stage, then just go back to focussing your attention on the present moment using your breathing and focussing on the sensations in your body.

Finally, you may like to extend this compassion to all living beings. *"May all beings be healthy and strong." "May all beings be happy (or peaceful)." "May all beings be filled with ease."*

Rest for a minute or so with your attention on your breathing and on your body. Notice any after-effects. Let any learnings integrate. As you rest now you can congratulate yourself on completing the exercise, no matter what your experience. You have acted out of compassion and shown courage.

Summary of Compassion to Self and Others - Me-Time Exercise 6 (10 mins)

1) Sit or lie down so that you are comfortably alert.
2) Pay attention to your breathing and then expand your attention to your whole body.
3) Start thought watching. Pay attention to sensations in your body. Notice any connection.
4) Breathe and be aware of your body.
5) Bring to mind a still lake on a sunny day. Imagine your body and mind as this still lake.
6) Gather your pebbles of compassion: *May I be healthy and strong, may I be happy, may I be filled with ease.*
7) Gently drop one pebble at a time into your lake. Watch for any reaction in your body. What thoughts, feelings or sensations if any arise?
8) Bring to mind a loved one. Tell them: *May you be healthy and strong, may you be happy, may you be filled with ease.* Notice

> any reaction. Breathe.
> **9)** Bring to mind a stranger. Follow the process in step 8.
> **10)** Bring to mind someone with whom you have been experiencing difficulties. Follow the process in step 8.
> **11)** Rest for a minute or so with your attention on your breathing and on your body. Pay attention to any after-effects.
> **12)** Congratulate yourself for your courage and compassion.

You may not have found this exercise particularly easy or comfortable. Some people find it really tricky to show themselves any love at all. It is almost as if we forget what it feels like to feel self compassion. Do not forget that your mind may have undergone years of hard treatment and tough love from you. All this is conditioning the mind to expect punishment. It may find it hard to accept kindness from you as a result.

At first, when I did this exercise I found it really awkward to even contemplate showing myself love. It felt a bit as though it was being egotistical (a limiting belief), which made me feel uneasy. It seemed unnecessary, *why do I need compassion?* I found it easier somehow to show compassion to other people and when I had done this it seemed to open something up inside me. I noticed that I was judging the process. As I focussed on dropping my pebbles in my lake I could imagine a feeling of warmth spreading throughout my body as the ripples spread out over the water. It felt a little like self acceptance to me.

Whatever your experience, keep practising. As you practise you will gradually break down the defenses that you have unconsciously erected around showing self-compassion, just as I did. You may also be aware now of any limiting beliefs that you have in this area.

Self compassion and self love are not the making of a monster, quite the reverse. Think of the positive messages that this is also sending to your saboteur. *May I be happy, may I be filled with ease.*

These are comforting and befriending messages that will settle and relax your saboteur.

As we explore sending compassion to other people and other beings, it helps in building our acceptance of them. It is much more difficult to show resentment towards something for which you have compassion. It is tricky to hold resistance towards something that you only have positive feelings for.

Compassion towards ourselves softens us, makes us more light-hearted. Compassion towards and acceptance of other people helps us build our relationships. It is difficult to hold negative feelings towards someone who wishes you well, shows you compassion and love.

Activities of well-being

We have opened up the possibility in your mind of showing yourself more respect, of being nicer to yourself. Now that we have done that it is worth assessing whether you have unconsciously constructed your everyday activities in a way that support you in having well-being and happiness or in ways that lack compassion towards your well-being.

Think about the things that you do during a normal week. Does your diet support your well-being? Do you exercise? What hobbies do you have? Which activities are you spending in doing mode (making withdrawals from your energy savings account) which in being mode (making deposits)? What thoughts do you start your day with? Do they support your well-being or not? Are you trapped in your autopilots or do you have sufficient variety in your life? Which relationships support or deplete your sense of well-being?

You can use the table below to note down your various activities:

Activity	Doing or Being? (D/B)	Supports Well-being? (Y/N)

Now you have your list, think about what you want more of in your life and what you want less of? What other things could you do that support your well-being? Commit to changing the way that you spend your time to facilitate your presence of mind and well-being.

Habit Breaker - Queuing Mindfully

Waiting in a queue can seem like a tortuous process sometimes. For people in a time pressured world it can become a very frustrating process, a complete waste of time. Now that you have learned the techniques of mindfulness, you can choose to see queuing in a different way.

Next time that you find yourself in a queue, you can start paying attention to any thoughts that start to build up. Start noticing any sensations, any frustration, any emotion that are forming in your body as you wait. What judgements do you start making about the queue, and about your experience? Be playful. See if you can see the funny side of your thinking?

As you observe thoughts, sensations and feelings, just in the same way as you have been doing in the various exercises, expand your focus of attention to include your breathing. Start seeing your thoughts as slides on the slideshow of your mind. Breathe into and out of the sensations. Notice the thoughts coming and going. Notice the sensations ebbing and flowing as you observe them and breathe into them.

Come back to focussing on your breathing and paying attention to the things that you can take in through your senses. Ground yourself in the present moment. See how this changes your experience.

Key Points

- We tend to be more critical of ourselves than we would ever be to other people.
- Our unconscious mind takes this self criticism personally. As we repeat things over and over in our heads we begin to believe our own self talk, this affects our sense of self worth.
- The next mindfulness exercise encourages us to be more compassionate to ourselves and to others.
- Once we gain self acceptance, then our self worth improves and inevitably this improves our health and happiness.
- If we have only positive thoughts for others, then we find that any resistance to them disappears.

CHAPTER 22

Turning towards your future

If you have been completing the exercises as you have been going through the book, as I have recommended, then you will be beginning to see some great rewards now. If you have come to this point and you are still to do the exercises then now is the time to go back and do them.

At this stage your awareness is at a good level. You have in mind all of the concepts, the theory, the reasons why the principles in this book will add value to your life in a big way for the long term. All of this is fresh in your mind. By doing your reading you have set up the neurological links in your mind and body that make change and improvement possible. They are all waiting to be used. Use them now. Get practising.

Neurological connections set up automatic thinking and behaviour processes: this is how we create habits. By imparting the knowledge as we have in this book we have challenged some of your long held beliefs and thinking. We have set up new neurological links that with repeated use will assist you in creating new habits and behaviours for yourself. I am sure that some of the information and concepts in this book will stay with you forever.

But if you do not use the knowledge soon, if you let the links lie dormant for a period of time, then the links will break and they will be of less use to you.

The best way to ensure that you continue to use these practices is to make them a part of your life, integrate them into your activities.

Mindfulness triggers

Think about all of the routine things that you do every day. You will generally do most routine things on autopilot simply because they are routine. Any of these activities give you the perfect opportunity to be present and mindful. Turning towards the future now you can use these activities as triggers for mindfulness:

Eating: The key is to cut down on distractions. When you sit down for a meal turn off your phone, turn off the TV, shut down your other electronic devices and focus on the pleasures of eating. Notice the textures, shapes and colours in your food. As you eat, savour every mouthful.

Showering: As you enter the shower open your mind up to the present moment. Notice the sounds of the water splashing onto the surfaces. As you test the temperature of the water become acutely aware of the feel of the water hitting your hand or foot. Step under the spray and see if you can feel the individual jets of water as they bounce off your skin. Smell the fragrance of the soap. Feel the softness of the soap suds as you rub them into your skin. What sensations do you feel?

Walking: Use walking as a way to connect with nature. What animals can you see? What different patterns of light can you notice on the objects and buildings around you? What can you smell? Focus on the world around you and your breathing. Use your breathing to ground you in the now.

Washing up/Ironing/Household chores: Household chores are the perfect opportunity to explore your levels of acceptance and resistance. What resistances do you feel as you contemplate the chores that you have to do? Notice any judgements, decisions, and beliefs that you have around doing the chores. Become mindful of your movements. Move deliberately, smooth out your movements. Make your chores into a gentle flow of movement, noticing as you move the feel of the things that you are touching. Enjoy noticing your breathing.

Listening: Listening is a great way to pay respect to another person. It says to them "I appreciate you." Focus 100% on just listening. Notice when you find yourself combining listening and planning what you are going to say in response. Notice when your mind wanders. Pay attention to any judgements that you are making of the things that the other person is saying, return to just listening.

Daily Mindfulness Practice

Work out a way to build some me-time into your daily schedule. Have a period of at least half an hour set aside just to practise the mindfulness exercises in this book and to write a journal on your progress. In your journal it is not important what you write down; just put down any thoughts that you are having, notes on what you noticed in your exercises, judgements, decisions and beliefs that you have discovered.

To start with you should plan to do each mindfulness exercise at least six times consecutively to really strengthen the neurological links that you are building before you move on to the next exercise. Once you are familiar with the exercises you can just decide to rotate them or decide on any one day which one you are going to practise depending on how you feel.

As you go about your day remember that you have tools available to you to assist you in becoming mindful and present, to reduce any stress that you are feeling or to ground you and relax you.

Use the technique of expanded awareness to clear your thoughts, become alert, reduce any inner chatter. Use the three minute breathing space exercise to break the cycles of anxiety and worry, increase your energy, refocus your attention, relax your mind processes and reassure your saboteur.

Review your values

Now is a great time to go back and redo the values exercise (starting on page 104). Your mind is changing all the time, we understand this now as neuroplasticity. The reading that you have done in this book and the exercises that you have been doing will have gently changed the shape of your brain. As your brain changes, so do your priorities.

Notice any changes in the order of your values. Have new values appeared on your list? You may well notice that more of your values point towards what you want as your future becomes more empowering for you.

Review your action plans. Bearing in mind what you want and what you now know about yourself, what actions can you take that will enable you to get there? Plan them into your diary.

Key Points

- Think about some of the routine tasks that you do every day. Make them into your mindfulness practices.
- Start making mindfulness a way of life.
- Plan daily me-time sessions into your diary.
- Review your values regularly.
- Do the exercises in this book now!

CHAPTER 23

Planning your future

You have all the tools at your disposal now to go ahead and create your future the way that you want it. You have the power and resources to create the results in life that you want. What is past is past, put it behind you now and step into the life that you want for yourself.

Every moment in time is there for you to savour. Every moment in time you get to decide what you focus on. Take the opportunity to spend every moment in time using your senses to the full.

Continue to see your thoughts as events, clouds, slides on the slideshow in your mind. Your thoughts are not you, they are created by you and you get to decide if you act upon them.

Whatever worries and anxieties you have, they are mind created thoughts, they are not reality. Reality is in the here and now. Reality is not the internal representations that you create using your mind filters, reality is the information that is available to you using your senses.

Whatever your past, whatever the future holds for you, your life is now. This moment is all that matters.

A future supported by your saboteur

Your unconscious mind is there to support you in your life in getting what you want. Your saboteur will always be there. It lives in the reptilian part of your brain. Your saboteur is a protection mechanism that will assist you in making the right decisions for you as long as you recognise its involvement in your life, as long as you befriend it and as long as you give it the right instructions.

You have the knowledge and skills to identify where your saboteur has possibly been detrimental to you in the past. This has only occurred through your lack of awareness. You will continue to notice your saboteur nudging you in certain directions in the future. Through being mindful of your judgements and thoughts you will continue to discover limiting beliefs and decisions that are signals from your saboteur.

As you reflect during your daily periods of self reflection and doing the mindfulness exercises you can ask yourself *"what challenges am I backing off from?"* You can see these things now in the full light of your awareness as involvement from your saboteur. Think logically *"Is this fear? Is the fear in proportion? Is there really anything to be fearful of?"* Smile to yourself knowingly as you see through your mental and psychological fears. Just remain playful and say to yourself *"I can see the truth. Thank you for protecting me. It is going to be ok."* Your saboteur will feel comforted by your attention, it will let you move on swiftly and easily with no resistance towards getting what you want.

Creating your future - Traveling on your Timeline

In order to assist you in getting your lights all on green, getting your life the way that you want it and creating the results that you want in life, we are going to introduce you to a final process and we are going to do a final exercise.

In this process we are going to use some of our understanding of how we create internal representations in our mind, and how our mind stores past and future memories to guide us in our behaviour, and our moods. We are going to use this knowledge to prepare our mind filters and our saboteur for the future that we want for ourselves.

As we discussed previously we each have a personal timeline in our mind. Our unconscious mind stores memories, past and future in this timeline so that they are easily retrievable for us and so that we can distinguish a chronological order in them.

The first thing that we need to do is to assist you in identifying the setup of your own timeline.

As the name *timeline* implies, we will be looking to ascertain some kind of line that you can be aware of and that links your past and future memories together. Because this timeline is stored in your unconscious mind, you may not be aware of it consciously and so you may not be absolutely certain as to how it looks. This is ok. Whichever way it is set up for you, or whichever way you think that it is set up is fine. Your participation in the process is more important than the details.

Most people find that whilst they are not absolutely sure at first, they get a feeling that their timeline is either from left to right, with their past on the left and their future on their right, or from back to front, with their past behind them and their future in front. It is the feeling or the inkling that we are after, not the certainty.

We are going to need you to trust signals from your unconscious mind in order to bring the timeline into your awareness. So if you do not know the answer to one of the questions below, then just trust your unconscious mind to provide you with an answer. If a possible answer springs to mind, then just take that as your signal.

1) Sit comfortably. This will only take a few moments. You may prefer to do this with your eyes closed.

2) Think of an event that happened to you six months or a year ago. Can you notice which direction that memory comes to you from? Do you have an inkling of where it might have come from?

   Take your finger and point in the direction of that memory.

3) Think of an event that happened a year ago. Where did that memory seem to come from? Where could it have come from? Point in that direction.

4) Continue going back in time getting memories from five, ten years ago, fifteen years ago, all the way back to early childhood. Note the location of each memory.

5) Now, do the same thing for the future. Think of something that will probably happen in the next six months to one year, two years, five years.

   Pay particular attention to which direction the "memory" or thought comes to you from. Take your finger and point in that direction.

   Can you notice that this memory originates in a different place from your past memories? Could it do?

   Your future usually appears in the opposite direction to your past.

6) Having located your past and future memories, now bring your thoughts to the present. Where do you locate the present?

   Note that your "present" appears in a different location from

> your past and future memories.
>
> 7) When you were pointing, where did you point to? Join up all the individual memories (and that includes the past and future "memories"). This is your personal timeline.

Did you get your timeline? Hopefully you did, but if you are still searching, then it may come to you later, for now just think of a way that you would like your timeline to be stored. Imagine a past and a future and a line in between with now in the middle.

Close your eyes for a second and bring your timeline to mind. See your past and your future. Notice internal representations in the memories on either side. You could think of them as individual slides on your timeline. Open your eyes.

In a moment I am going to ask you to think of a goal for your future. You are going to close your eyes again and you are going to bring your timeline back into your mind's eye. You are going to float up above your timeline and out into your future. From this position in your future and above your timeline you are going to drop the internal representation of your goal so that it floats gently down into your timeline. You will watch as the act of doing this changes all of the memories and internal representations from this future moment in time all the way back to now. You are then going to float back from this position back to and down into now.

> 1) First of all then, you are going to get a goal for your future. What is the one thing that you would like for your future that will make the biggest difference to your happiness and your destiny? Make sure that it is something that you and only you have control over. Imagine what actions that you need to take in order to get it. What is a realistic timescale for achieving these actions and getting your goal?
>
> 2) Once you have your goal in mind, then I need you to see

yourself achieving it. So go ahead and imagine yourself achieving it. What can you see? What do you feel? What do you hear as you are achieving it? Which people are around you? What are they saying to you? As you get the picture in mind of you achieving your goal, make sure that you put yourself in the picture so that you actually see yourself achieving it. So, step out of the picture and see your body in the picture. Notice how you appear. Notice what you are doing. Notice how you are feeling. Really turn up the brightness on the picture, make the colours vivid, so that it looks just right and is perfectly clear in your mind.

3) When you have your internal representation just the way that you want it, then close your eyes if you still have them open and bring your timeline back into mind. Float gently up into the air so that you are up above your timeline.

4) From above your timeline turn towards the future and look out into your future. Start floating out towards your future.

5) Notice the time in your future where you are going to be achieving your goal. Stop above that time.

6) Look down into your timeline and as you do that just release your grip on the internal representation of you achieving your goal. As you release your grip, just see it floating gently down into your timeline.

7) See your internal representation slotting into your timeline just in the right place. As your goal comes to rest in your timeline notice how all of the existing slides, all of your future memories from this point back to now, start realigning themselves. Notice how all of the slides start adjusting to make room for and accommodate this new goal. The simple act of placing this goal in your future changes the dynamic of your future. Notice how great it looks.

8) When you are ready. From your position out in the future

> and above your timeline, float back to now nice and slowly, nice and gently.

Your lights are all on green. How does it feel now knowing that your future is perfectly set up to achieve your most empowering goal? It feels great, doesn't it?

You can go ahead and repeat this exercise for any other goals or objectives that you have now or at any time in the future.

Any time that you find yourself getting anxious and worrying you can just close your eyes and float up above your timeline. Float out into your future to just past the time of the event that you are worrying or anxious about. See events turning out successfully for you. Nothing to worry about. No need to be anxious. Enjoy the present moment.

You now have the mind management tools to get the results that you want in life. Spend your time in the now. Whenever you notice that you are in doing mode and thinking is taking over, use the anchors that we have set up with your breath to bring you back to the present moment.

Allocate specific times during your day to do your planning and reviewing, know that having done this you have no need to spend any other time in past and future thinking. Your time is now, the present moment is all that you have and all that is important. Think and act as though you are one of the greatest people on this planet because you are. You are unique, you are amazing, you have an incredibly powerful tool at your disposal, use it to create the life that you deserve.

...and so it was that I was sat in my car by the side of the road looking at the beautiful scenery around me, the sun coming up on the horizon, the mist gently rising from the damp ground, observing the wildlife excitedly going about their morning. I realised that I had stumbled across the thing that I was missing in my life. Presence of mind. In this moment of lucidity it dawned on me that one day will be my last. I thought about my destiny and I thought about the way that I was living my life. *When I am on my deathbed then, what will be the most important things to me about the way that I lived my life?*

I thought, *if these things are going to be the most important thing in the end, then why not make them the most important things now?*

INDEX

acceptance 92, 94, 238, 243-244, 251-252, 254, 257

addictions 74-76, 84

amygdala 23

Angelou, Maya 18

anger 13, 21-23, 30, 41, 54-55, 88, 91, 93, 203, 222

anxiety 67, 86-94, 120, 129, 138, 141, 187

Apple Inc 51, 68

astronomy 34-37

attitude 50, 108, 113, 142, 159

auditory 19

automatic pilot 150, 168, 182

autopilot 157, 160-164, 168, 171-172, 184-185, 213, 215, 224, 242, 252, 256

Bannister, Roger 72

befriending 141, 207, 234-244

behaviour 23-27, 41-43, 47-49, 52-56, 74-78, 82-84, 88, 90, 94, 98,99, 101, 105, 113, 163-164, 171, 184, 200, 218-219, 222, 225, 236, 247, 255, 261

Beck, Aaron 90

Being Mode 147-160, 173-174, 178, 185, 194-196, 198, 203, 206, 215, 218

beliefs 25-26, 29, 37, 50, 54-55, 78, 98-102, 108-109, 114, 152, 217-225, 230, 236, 243, 251, 257,260
false 69, 215, 217-219

blood Pressure 47, 89, 142

body & breath 173-185, 194, 206, 211, 248

body & mind 186-199, 248, 250

Body Scan 189-195, 204

Breathing Space Exercise 203-205

cancer 62, 142

candle 21-22

Cantbebotheredyitis 92

categorise 52

CBT (See Cognitive Behavioural Therapy)

INDEX

change 57-60, 64, 67-70, 73, 88, 92, 100, 103, 106,108-110, 113, 123, 129, 138-140, 147, 150, 154, 163, 173, 183-185, 204-206, 208, 222-223, 228, 239-240, 254, 258, 263-264

Chauying, J Jen 60

chemicals 13, 31-32, 39, 63-64, 84, 86, 87, 89- 93, 112, 154

chess 15,16

children 17, 21, 40, 54, 55, 92, 138, 224

chocolate 38
    addiction 75-76
    Chocolate Exercise 164-172

Chopra, Deepak 64

chunks (chunking) 27-28, 50-52, 163-164, 211

coaching 6, 30, 72, 100, 247

Cognitive Behavioural Therapy 90

Columbus, Christopher 67

comfort zone 68-73, 100, 110, 184

compassion 141, 143, 152, 179, 212, 245-254

confidence 2, 67, 81, 92, 122

conscious processes 3-4

cortisol 87, 89, 112

counselling 30, 62, 90

crime 30, 69

criticise 78, 245

Dali, Salvador 51

death 30, 33, 90-91, 94, 200, 238, 266

decisions 25, 27, 44, 48, 50, 54, 58, 67-68, 71, 73-74, 101, 121, 142, 159, 171, 188, 218, 232-233, 236, 238, 257, 260
    limiting 219-221, 230, 232

defensive (being) 78-84, 108, 245

deletion 50-51, 53, 54, 78, 102, 142, 218

depression 31, 86-94, 138

destiny 71, 103, 148, 263, 266

difficulties 238-243, 250-251

distortion 51-54, 78, 102, 142, 218

distraction 136, 159, 164, 171, 256

Doing Mode 146-160, 170-171, 178, 185, 194-199, 202, 211, 231, 252, 265

dopamine 63, 91, 112

dreams 9, 16, 51, 61, 66, 70
    day-dreaming 178, 180, 181, 193

embracing 186, 242

emotions, domain of 20-23
    negative 29- 31, 86-94, 117, 120, 126, 188, 242

Encyclopedia Britannica 43

energy 3, 9, 28, 31, 33, 47, 52, 62, 64, 75, 87, 92, 94, 153, 164,

INDEX

195, 201, 213, 237, 245, 252, 258

energise 47, 122, 125, 128, 130, 203, 242

Ennis-Hill, Jessica 53

evolution 11-12, 65, 136, 268

exercise 31, 60 63, 90-91, 93
high 63

expanded awareness 160, 198, 203, 258
exercise 154-156

failure 66-67, 78, 90, 94, 99, 145, 159, 201

fear 13, 21-24, 30-31, 33, 41, 45, 51, 65-73, 80-81, 87-88, 93, 111, 116, 121, 135, 140, 145, 152, 179, 187-188, 201-202, 225, 230-231, 241, 243, 260

Ferguson, Sir Alex 4

fight or flight 12, 29, 41, 65-66, 73, 77, 80, 82, 87, 89, 93, 121, 145, 152, 170, 180, 201, 234, 236

generalisation 52-54, 78, 102, 142, 218

genetics 59, 99

goals 10, 59, 69, 74, 93, 112, 125, 129, 144, 145-146, 150, 152-153, 201-202, 265

growth 27, 69, 89, 114

guilt 9, 10, 13, 30, 88, 91, 218, 220, 221, 240

gustatory 19

habits 23-29, 39, 41, 56, 74, 88, 90, 93, 113, 129, 163- 164, 168, 171, 174, 255

Habit Breaker 156-158, 184, 197, 212, 232, 253

Halley's Comet 34-37

happiness 2-3, 5, 31, 63-64, 70-71, 84, 86, 93, 98, 99, 106, 138, 141, 142, 154, 158, 216, 252

helping people 98-99

holiday 8, 18, 138, 144, 148-149, 187, 217, 235

Holmes, Oliver Wendell 58

household chores 76-77, 120, 257

hurt 13, 30, 65-66, 83, 88, 91

hypnosis 28, 60

illness 31-32, 87, 238

immune system 62, 87, 89, 142

impact 18, 22, 41, 54, 63, 107, 144, 145, 160, 188, 200, 201, 213, 219, 245, 249

Imprint Period 99

intention 21, 25, 29, 31, 74, 76, 82-85, 88, 93, 166, 197, 198, 219

INDEX

internal representations 40, 44-45, 47, 49, 50, 98, 117, 119, 120, 125, 126, 129, 201, 218, 259, 261, 263

iPad 68

irritation 78-79

Jobs, Steve, 51, 68

journal 97, 113, 257

judgement 55, 69, 142, 150-151, 159, 188, 199, 218-219, 231, 233, 236-238, 249, 253, 257, 260

kinaesthetic 19

Kingfisher 45

leader 4, 67

learning 26-27, 36-39, 53, 100, 141

Limbic System 12, 13, 21

liver 32, 62

Lombardi, Vince 4

lose weight 110-112

MacLean, Dr Paul 11, 12

Massey, Morris 99

Me-time mindfulness exercises 173-174, 194, 198, 202, 257-258
Breath & Body 175
Body Scan 189
Mindfulness in Movement 206
Silence, Sounds & Thoughts 226
Exploring Resistance & Difficulties 238
Compassion to Self & Others 247

Meiwes, Armin 83

memory 17-20, 27-30, 36, 37, 40, 41, 44, 45, 49, 50, 53, 60, 61, 78, 101, 113, 117, 119-121, 125, 141-143, 151, 152, 173, 183, 217, 260-262

mental suffering 65-66

mice 59-60

Miller, George 50

mind filtering 49, 54-56, 218

mind management skills 3-5, 31

mind wandering 156, 178-180, 193-194

model of the world 41, 43, 50-51, 90

motivation 12, 98, 100, 110-116, 123, 125-130, 142, 200-202, 213, 214

negatives 39-40, 76, 200, 213

neglect 9, 54, 77, 186, 199, 213

Neocortex 13, 23, 140

nervous system 59, 63

INDEX

neurological connection 32, 186, 255
    links 121-123, 129, 179, 237, 255, 257
    networks 154

neuron 57-64, 154

neuroplasticity 57-60, 64, 258

neuroscience 59

neurotransmitter 63, 89, 91

nightmares 22

NLP (Neuro-Linguistic Programming) 7

olfactory 19

overwhelm 24, 48-49, 71, 164, 167, 171

past events 20, 25, 30-31, 158

patterns 15-22, 27, 38, 41, 44, 52, 53, 66, 75, 90, 94, 121, 135, 164, 171, 182-184, 189, 213, 221, 230, 233, 247, 256

perception 34-38, 41, 73, 77-78, 82, 83, 93, 98, 243
    projecting 53, 56

phobias 22

positive intention 76, 82-85, 88, 93, 219

Potato Crisp exercise 156-157

potential 65, 69

procrastination 76-77, 84, 126

prioritising 10, 44, 100

problem solving 7, 25, 143, 144, 151, 186, 237

programming 15, 17, 52, 219

psychological pain 65-66

queuing 253

rabbit 18-19, 28

relationships 3, 29, 72, 78, 84, 100, 107, 142, 153, 252

relaxation 62, 94, 112-113

repetition 26-27, 39, 41, 168

Reptilian Complex 12, 13
    Brain 68, 72, 74, 82, 84, 170, 260

resistance 68-69, 234-244, 252, 254, 257, 260

responsibility 58-59, 70, 187

rules 52, 66, 98-102, 221-225, 232-233, 236, 243

saboteur (inner) 65-85, 93, 107-113, 116, 123, 124, 129, 130, 135-136, 140-141, 145-146, 152, 159, 164, 168, 170, 171, 184, 185, 187, 188, 196, 198, 201-202, 205, 211-252, 258, 260-261

sadness 13, 30, 65, 88, 91, 217

selective attention 51

INDEX

self care 92

self deception 9, 144

self harm 30, 247

self talk 140, 147, 155, 156, 160, 245-247, 254

sensory aspects 125
    data 22
    delights 198
    experience 160, 170, 172, 238
    information 20

seratonin 63, 89

Simmonton, Dr 62

silence 134, 180, 224-232, 236

Simpson, Joe 32-33

smoking 40

spiders 22

state of mind 45-47, 49, 129, 142, 145, 152, 218, 219

stress 43, 56, 64, 86-94, 136, 138, 141, 147, 148, 159, 174, 187-188, 194, 202, 206, 212, 214, 221-223, 250, 258
    reduction 112-113

symbols 15-22, 27, 38, 40-41, 52

synaptic gap 63

tennis 4, 16

therapy 30, 90

timeline 19-20, 260-265

Traits (7) of Doing and Being 150-154

triggers 29, 41, 68, 77-79, 121-123, 142, 171, 173, 225, 256

Triune Brain 11-13

unconscious processes 3-5, 169, 224, 226

unknown 68-69, 72, 110, 145

unwanted behaviour 49, 74-78, 82, 84, 164

values 9, 10, 25, 26, 37, 50, 98-130, 138, 216, 218-219, 224, 258

visual 19, 44, 154
    visualise 18, 62, 130, 175, 180
    visual rehearsal 122

weather systems 183

well-being 63-64, 89, 98, 113, 138, 141, 153, 188, 252-253

wool 15

worry 88-94, 120-121, 129-130, 146, 153, 158, 174-177, 183, 185, 187, 193-194, 202, 214, 222, 225-226, 231, 240, 258, 265

wound 13, 32

About Anthony Beardsell

Anthony Beardsell is a professional coach and trainer specialising in the fields of NLP, Leadership and Coaching. He works with a variety of individuals and organisations worldwide to assist them in creating success and growing towards their potential. He holds a degree in French, Spanish and Economics and is a Master Trainer and Master Practitioner of NLP.

Based in Sheffield, England, Anthony owns and runs Excellence Assured Ltd. Excellence Assured provide a platform for Anthony to offer his coaching and training services and its website, http://excellenceassured.com is home to his blog.

Anthony says: "As a coach and through my training courses I come across people searching for answers as to how to change their thinking and behaviour to get better results. Typically they want to create less stress for themselves, improve their levels of success and happiness. Through my knowledge of NLP and Mindfulness I am able to assist them in discovering the answers to these questions."

Upon attaining his degree, Anthony spent twenty years working in the field of consultancy, and sales management in the UK financial services sector. It was through his success in working with teams and individuals in this field that Anthony built his passion for coaching and training.

In addition to his coaching, Anthony has produced a series of NLP, Leadership, Mindfulness and Coaching training courses that are available online to help people to understand why they think and act as they do, create better results for themselves and work with others.

He has put together a model of thinking and a set of techniques that anyone can use to lead them to better mind management and more mindful living, thus creating improved happiness, less stress, and greater levels of success. It is this model that he shares in this book.

Resources in Mindfulness and NLP

Excellence Assured Ltd offers a complete range of learning tools and coaching services to help you in getting your life the way that you want it.

Online Training Courses - Presented by Anthony Beardsell

Mindfulness
The full multimedia version of our Mind Management & Mindfulness programme.
Videos, audio, fully illustrated manual.
Including an eight week guided Mindfulness programme

NLP Certification Training Courses
- NLP Practitioner
- NLP Master Practitioner
- NLP Trainer

Leadership Training Courses
- Game Changing Leadership
- Leadership Development

Coaching Training Course
- Coaching

Coaching

Work towards getting the results that you want and realising your potential with face to face and Skype coaching from Anthony Beardsell:

To book Anthony, visit http://excellenceassured.com or contact us on +44 (0)845 257 0053.

Printed in Great Britain
by Amazon